WarFair4.com The Day the Markets stood *still* *1.1.1….*

Standard Oil Co. by Pablo Neruda, Canto General, 1940

Ebook formatting by www.ebooklaunch.com

WF4.2.

WarFair4.1: The Day the Market(s) stood *still*...

M.Stow

Contents

'It has been said that love of money is the root of (many) evil(s) and a wandering from the path which has brought-upon us much pain. The lack (need) of money is so quite as truly.' **Samuel Butler** (1835-1902 ME) EREWHON Ch. 20 (amended after: The Old Testament: 1Timothy, and before **Mark Twain** (Mark Twain's Notebook 1909 ME).

'If the man and the woman bear their fair share of work, they have a right to their fair share of all that is produced by all, and that share is enough to secure them well-being.' **Petr Kropotkin** (1842 - 1921) The Conquest of Bread; Mutual Aid: A Factor of Evolution.

The-train engine moved slowly out from the glass and steel raised slab of the new edge-of-Town main-line high-speed railway-platform, running alongside the banking blank back of high-street shops, and the station car-park, awaiting return. Into harvested-fields and open-grazed pastures below remaining precipitous pine-forest alongside planted poplar windbreak shielded river road and rail.

Through the trees, the new days' sun appeared, speared, blinking-awake burst through the carriage breaking beyond the blue grey staged and staggered, rolled and ranged. From the east-peaked settling yellow-orange onto the western-hills. Shadow-flanking purple-green valleys, and upcountry the grid-framed farmed plains, where the day was already begun.

Grey-blue steam lifted across a drying-up estuary in thin rain spluttering over an elevated iron-riveted painted girder-bridge, built-on pillars of a deep-red local stone and brickwork, arched and breached.

With the Suns'-rays the train rattled-on emergent, as through a fog over a beached river, onto the other-side of a ravenous gaping-gorge.

Over-spilling through the outskirts of a more recently built-up ancient sea-harbour and river port and suburban edge-of-Town. High-Rise Housing-Project, Industrial-Units, Business-Park, and Shopping-Mall. Home-Furniture and Motor-Car showrooms. Salesrooms, cheap-hotel and motel linked razor-wire fenced, chained-in. A horse-paddock, gated and padlocked, adjacent to a blue-green to red-waiting train-crossing signal. Freight-Train, privileged-over passenger passaged prerogative *thundering-by...*

The Passenger Commuter-Train trundling along for now, beside a chequered yellow and black no entry arterial hot tar-road weighted heavy and ever busy with 'bus and coach, cycle and motor cycle. Engine chassis and trailer caravan motor-home articulated jugger-naut. Stocks and Goods container shipments onboard onto and beneath the over passing concrete-highway into and out of Town. All traffic travelling with *almost* one accord: to-and-from galvanized corrugated iron steel and zinc tin roofing roved between brick and-cinderblock doorways, loading and un-loading bays beneath open canopy entrance letter and number laser bar-coded and secured to the outside world unseen windowless between effluence extracting hot air white-grey belching cooling-tower pylon-linking gas-welding workshop engineering factory plastic-moulded metal-machine worked and handmade goods processed food, and furniture, packaged, warehoused, and shipped0 to-and-from City Ports and Portals' virtually co-modifying in-vestment in-return stockyards stacked-up and in exchange-value assured awaiting transport to-and-from: Home and Abroad…

Part One: The Day the Markets stood still…

1. <u>She.</u>

'It's like living in a rabbit-hutch' She often said metaphorically, and He replied with a shrug, with n*othing to say in reply. It was; and it would take long enough to pay for. Four rooms. Eight floors up, eight flights of long turning concrete-stairs fire-doors missing and for escape for when the unreliable elevators did not function an open balcony passageway at the front, looking over the street below, now starting to become busy with traffic. They had lived with his parents for a time, and then after they were married in a small rented flat in The City, before they needed to afford somewhere to live together, and to bring-up their two small children.*

They *saved, and with some financial help from a relative (deceased) they had managed to get this place when the housing-market was 'buoyant' and mortgages easy to get. The Home was bought with a loan, a promissory note, deposited and co-lateraled together with the home itself. They were afloat. Both worked to pay-off the loan which although it was supposed to reduce each year did not seem ever to keep up with pay and prices.*

The Home-Loan would anyway be paid-off many times over if they were ever to pay-off the debt. If this place was ever to become their own. If they managed to keep paying-off the loan for the 'Shelter from the Storm', as they called Their-Home. That they did not actuarily now own, and may not ever, actually own, lose-lose. To sell-back at Market Price, the difference between the buying-price and selling-price of which they would have lost completely to The Bank...The Mortgage Company. Their home re-possessed a two-bedroom apartment, she thought of: *kitchen, lounge, shower-bathroom toilet and tiny balcony onto the world below, between them and the sky above.*

Each day, each month, and each successive year into the un-thinkable future. Two-thirds of two-lifetimes, two-thirds every month of what they were both paid, together. She did the household accounts, and She knew.

The Home. The Loan Would have been paid for several times over by the time if ever it became their own owned Home and The Childrens' and perhaps even their Grand- Childrens' by the time the shared building was made uninhabitable con.demned de-molished damned the-land free-held lease-back extended more con.densed re-build landed-property to someone else royal regal imperialistic e-stately government un-earned tax-rent win-win.

But, that is the nature of the human animal, is it not?

To do over, and be done over to, again and again She-*thought*: we-*want more and more for less and less* and in the *quiet*-mind wandering moment of pillared door, a room, a table *a bed let go and a bed sheet left behind, ready to be buried with perhaps as they did in the olden-times...shrouded* as now by thin curtains pulled-back.

Each-Day: like a two-steps forward and then backwards step earned worked to pay-off the loan on the house and to pay for food and bills and extras, clothes, and nights out, occasionally. Maybe once a month, or not at all.

Then He had been laid-off work at The-Bakery. Three-day-week, and three days wages.

The Home mortgage was re-negotiated, and they continued struggling to pay-off the loan and other loans credited as directly debited debt from what they both earned together. There was never an issue of who would earn more, and be the main bread-winner; and who would do the most caring of each other, and the children the unpaid responsibilities shared around the home and in the world of work, shopping and holidays and other friends and family out-
there. All in-debted in-credit.

All in-credit in-debted.

They were equal, without even having to think about it or confront societies and others' false expectations of gender and families. They were equal in-credit and in-debted, and supported each other's frail and fragile egos with a natural equanimity respectful and loving, each contributing their best and differently not in-differently to make the whole, whole.

'It's not all doom and gloom...bills to pay, rent to make.' she did often think, and he tried not to think on it. *The homely claustrophobia only had to be relieved by going out. To the cinema, to a bar or restaurant. But that was not very often. De-finitely now there were children as well. Seldom did extras make their mark, clothes bought carefully a piece at a time, replacement rather than extravagance.*

The cupboards filled with groceries and emptied by the time the next weeks shopping is needed and the next weeks earnings already spent.

She was awake, first this morning, and she got up from the bed on which he still lay awake but not yet awake enough to leave its' night-time *warmth*. She went through to the next room. The bedroom led across the narrow-passage to the living room, which led directly to the tiny gallery kitchen and balcony on one side and door to the front room on the other. Except it wasn't the front-room, exactly, only *like* the 'front-room' of her childhood *playing on the street and door directly to the rugged ragged matted smell of cooking from the stone-walled white-washed country kitchen two bedrooms and a closet room to flush away a basin of water from the kitchen sink into the slurry sump, where you could hear it 'slurry' all the way down. All the way down to replace water from the outside tap pumped up from the well re-filling the fired china clay bowl and zinc-metal bucket, ready for the next use. At night-time bedtime children first, then the adults. Rats nested runs, beetles and cockroaches were kept away by the domesticated cats and dogs that shared the yard and house. With horses at the local stables to ride at week-ends, and Holy Days. Each week, several times into the market town for food supplies, and the children's treats. Their whole world a Living Market Place, of Work and Play.*

Now, great enclosed parked superstores and supermarkets and factory outlet warehouse. Where goods are now trans-ported she thought of: *to and from and by hand and foot and motor vehicle train massive tanker and flight container-*

shipping from the docks and airport, at the city harbour hub humming away, remote yet directing everyday life, everywhere.

Passenger and cargo. The affordable flight, to get away from it all: a change; a necessary move, once in a while, not every year but to visit family here and there and elsewhere, or else you'd go stir-crazy. Do a night-time flit, leave the rent, the mortgage, unpaid. Only, to otherwise keep on fighting for the next bargain cheapest *within budget* to get through to the next day and the day after that.

When debts and fines could not be paid, the debt- collector. Bailiffs, The-Auctioneer: selling- off of the personal possessions, and then sold-out: the personal and public. The laptop computer on-*sleep* and awakened, opened, placed on the table, booted-up and she blogged instantaneously *her*-thoughts: *'We all need a roof over our heads and to put Food on the Table!'* without any other word, or contextual continuity that did not remain obvious to this early morning. *Everyone, and anyone in the same and similar circumstances* getting the similarly same hastily tapped-out message; *ex-cluding those without phone-tablet, food or home, and those with patently far too-much who had admin.-staff appointed to work for them to-mulch greed and indifference to all other and all else* and her *thought* continued in the context of the mindful moment *and that which we all have to pay extortionately excoriatingly for over and again even when the food is eaten and the crap washed away there remains a nasty-taste. A stain the original wages as sin sweated over day upon day and the loans ever in negative equity! To who? Them! Extortionate interest volatile prices and pay*... looking-up and down again now, not in-dejection but circumspection against ever apparent possible too likely failure with desperate optimism toward un-realistic perfectionism.

Below mechanized traffic building-up soon into a busy rush-hour congestion.

Cars and buses, bicycles, motorbike motorized delivery-truck *from here only another view from two-sides and every side* the bedrooms along the passage corridor the sleeping children, slept. Earlier peeked into *soundless in im-perfectly re-collected beautiful dream, anxious concern or dreamless sleep seeming startling worrying death*-checked for breathing. Crossing from night into daytime TV remotely automatically tuned-in turned-on confirmation, that *life goes on…*

The *living*-room as she entered, bore all the chatter and the silence of one who listens. Still and safe, cosy, and secure. The other rooms took over the emotions and needs: sleep and food, love, and arguments. The central room, the central chamber, looked-on and awaited eventual, almost inevitable, but never certain, re-conciliation and rest. Indulged in social events, noisy chatter, and quiet evenings indoors.

The furniture was adequate and filled the room. Table, chairs, television, a drawer, and shelved cabinet standing against a wall, displaying various icons. Family photographs in frames, a portrait of a film star, or a print of a famous oil painting. Ornaments, statuettes, figures of worship and of novelty. The furniture, the infrastructure, from the livelihoods, and eventually the roof over our heads *in over our heads heard* as if originally spoken. There were unopened envelopes and cajoling leaflet advertisement: *Kill your debts! Die debts!* She *thought*-of letters and bills for payment, propped up behind a ticking clock. There was a picture postcard from someone-else's holiday forming a picturesque frontage to hide the stack of demands for reply and payment which lay beyond. She drew back the curtains and looked out of the window across the balcony, with its' un-flowering plants growing in flower-pots. There was a real still rising *mistiness* outside from the early morning warming; and she gazed over an area where many lived, and it seemed to her, this morning, where they too just lived out their lives: *day to day, week to week. They too thought to themselves* as She looked-out onto the dawn of a gradually opening new day *that the world must have always been this way.*

2. They.

They had stayed together and with two little ones, one of each, girl, and boy, by the time they're both about to be in school, they could not risk another to bring up, and the cost of it. They only hoped they would hold on to their jobs and worked hard. Difficult hours, and some days-off. Where the rotas didn't work-out for childcare, family or neighbours, parents now friends of the children's friends who lived conveniently nearby, the social network from the cradle to school to work to death...

They had met when things were starting to get a bit tight, to get difficult again. Meaning the situation for most working families, for those looking for work and *those in work, things had not got any better or any-*easier *really during the so-called 'good-times' and both- parents were needed in-credit and debt to work to help-keep the family going-on.*

Voluntary social-networks anti-social all the more significant re-creation rec.(i)procal: Shared-Care and Circles of Support. With child and adult interaction social and meaningful. Shared-Lives. They had both kept their jobs in more or less 'essential services' although not without the job-cuts, never the-less, ever the less, never the more, when things got difficult all a-round.

When the Bakery Factory where He and Family worked, went on three-days week, and pay to match. He, had more time to be with the children, and helped the same with her awkward *shift-work at the garment factory, and later She at the hospital, for the Children, then training there, working there. He had done some building work on the odd-days, to fill-in. She had done some shop-work and garment-making before all the Shop Jobs' 'Retail', were filled, and not-hiring. Not selling either. Queues at the cash-tills. To no-one at the field tills, no-one at the fields to till, filed for bankruptcy they had moved to his folks in The City then: suburbs really, inner-urban, something-like-that...*

His mother had worked at The Old Mill and got her a job there; and then him at The Bakers' Factory, at the top of the road.

When and where. The area they had moved-to. With Family and friendly neighbours nearby there: People, their people. They had moved in together and... His fathers' family had been transient transitory migrant millers, corn wheat rice and grain, local food gypsies own owned land and business machinery, hiring-out maintenance, and repair. Finding and digging the wells' water. Oil from the oil-swamp, clay brick- building and tarmac road, pave-laying.

Growing taking fruits and nuts, from the side of vegetable and allotment gardens, land-work and sold fair income sold-on on the roadways everywhere when in season.

They did well enough. Moving around farm to farm, funnily enough she thought *like Business-People nowadays do…l*ooking across the roads, below, leading to The City.

To: The Airport *to visit:* Sales-People *to the* Re-tail Outlets*'* Shops of the World*: in other words:* Big and little medium-sized down-sizing out-sourcing Business-Communityies' so-called c*ommuting by-airplane as well they might as of privilege if they could afford-to… why-not?*

To: go on Holiday. Abroad. They *thems themselves to meet Business-Clients Meetings' her(e) and there and everywhere. Populated: Cities all over to do deals on a Global-Scale massive then worth millions, now worth billions and trillions of whatever the currency.*

Sometimes-dealing even unevenly, unbalanced, in the local and World-Fiat Corporate-Currencies' bit-coins that's all for themselves.

They took on a Shop, Family-Bank loan to rent and stock and share.

In the past *when the work dried-up, landfill, polluted wells and rivers and seas and Oceans. His' family 'moved along' as they were constantly told:*

'Move-On.' And:

'Now!'

Or, they stayed enabled with their own-owned or owed Home-Stores' shares of the crops of the fields and water natural and free from the clean water-well. Waited, and looked for more or different labour...

She thought *of them, her own family, and His' families Out of Work they always found something. Fed them-selves from gardens and small farmyards when and where; and when the work was finished, they moved-on.*

When the Great-Corporate moved-in, took over, bought and sold-off Master-Slavery style, re-cruiting capturing sometimes for crimes unrecognised accused of along the roads and waterways they, her family, had a farm in the countryside for a while, and the in-law parents, lived there.

Her family through the Industrial now *Techno-Future*: The Soul of The City. Only, tumultuous-Towns and vicious-Villages. *Across the-River, across the tram-tracks and railway, by the station The* Heart of the City. The Financial-Quarter. *Settling-in. The-City. They always on the-edges, the peripheryies' walled and castellated. Transport and Trade-hub and thronged and His parents self employed, their own bosses contractors worked-out on the* Building Sites *of Towering Sky-Scrapers lining The River, and lit-up, like their soon to be shared DNA from the angling energising* Solar-Sun.

Her-Family employed, then not their own owned not-owed or owing boss nevermind Big-Boss. Both, though(t) as themselves, unknown to each other then.

Then, on some land, renting, from their pay then they, He and She, eventually buying: Home-Owners, now. Investors in their own future in bricks and mortar and their children's children, and theirs' owned, in re-turn for pay, not like-rent capable of being and being dis-owned lost mislaid and abandoned not strictly speaking owned, anyway but for the Mortgage Corporations and Companies' owned, and now: The-Bank(s). Building and Maintenance Trades. Education and their *Good-Health Taxied to meetings and desks…Home-Work and Out-working: the Home-Owners and Private and Publicly Rented-Sector: Social-Housing Association(s) and:* Gig: Market- Economy: 1%. To: 9%. To: 90% All *self-Employed all of us selfies sales' advert(i)sing ourselves tax-paying and claiming on-costs and prices-up and never-down depending on what side of the Power-Play had been Won-lost. Every milli-second playing-out and in-relationship(s) then&now to each-other…* Soon the hire-purchase television was blaring as usual in the morning. In the main- room that was empty again for the moment and beyond where she was nowdressing hurriedly, and he was brushing his hair frantically. There was the sound of children getting washed and dressed, with incessant commentary and conversation to each other, and any other, or just to themselves. To each other a one-way argument. Older to *younger* incited over some triviality, shouted back in frustration. At that point the only-game-in-town, and to be fought-out until one of them is crying, and the other shouting-the-odds; before calm is brought. *Evens* by one or the other parent, *super-vising*, managing, supposedly, to each-other, at least while they all got ready for work, school and pre-school&nursery.

The sound of the kitchen kettle screaming on the fire cook-top induction hot-plate hob and pixelated digital television advertisements conveying to deaf-ears and blind-eyes but re-ceptive memory:

'The Best in the World.' Or:

'Longer-lasting' or whatever the dubious selling point perhaps to be *unconsciously* recalled later that day, at the supermarket.

At present the adverts seemed to be of no avail, both rushed to get the children to school, and themselves out to work. To earn the pay that would pay the prices at *the* - later that day:

'Where is my shirt?' he called:

'Where you last put it!' she retorted as She entered the living room. She found her shoes under a chair and stopped in front of the television. The networked advertisements ended and the programme returned to the main story of the day:

'Today there is no money to pay share dividends, or to buy shares with…' She flicked a channel and got:

'Group and Individual Share Prices have collapsed or become so high that they have become worthless confidence has collapsed debt un-diminished…'

Then:

'Price increases have been blamed. Increases in pay and pensions have been blamed. Increases in Bank-Business Personal-Investment (*I*)nterest-rates' *maximizing* excessive Profit-levels at any-cost have been blamed. Each of these has pushed share Prices ever upwards. As Share-Prices and Shop-Prices overtake the customers' Ability to Pay and the ability to pay pushes prices-up pay-down…'

'Never pay-up! Or prices-down!'

She spoke to no-one in particular as she typed-in she saw see-sawing sea-crossing:

< Costs in-crease: nnn/NNN…

> Profit-margins narrowed: NNN/nnn/…

< Presidential-Corporate Mandate Historic-ally re-captured only by increases in tax-rates for most in sales and property taxes with decreases for the most wealthy re-lative to inheritance and corporation in excess of reduced ceiling Interest-rates on banking and other loans have pushed share-prices-up further in anticipation of firmer-Profits at the expense of customers' and voters' good-will.' and labor workers and those unable to work and earn decent…desending…' and a view passed across the screen to locked Factory-Gates and closed-down Hospital corridor(s)…

Then:

'Increased profits at the expense of workers where great global corporations benefit in the developed world. Under-developed worlds' trade agreements through World Trade Organisation environmental protection. Global trade agreements setting prices high and low some with no medicine too expensive hurts average workers without best labour standard unfair advantage to those organised or move abroad work property regulations dropped in-face of foreign bargaining power with worst business record on-record: list:…*cheaper* improve profitability alone works for everybody not just those at the top!

Tax breaks benefit whole economy more investment creating jobs and spending gig economy tech.-bubble burst property rights protected abroad investment job destruction disrupt adapt trade and employment arbitration outside of health safety environmental protections costs reimbursed energy treaty allow good-economics equals what actually happens in theory forecasting great things what things? Practicing people in control can *fight*-back use examples like plutonium in baby cereals vaccine in leaf lettuce…soft-propaganda works hard only if necessary…doing well at the time no better no worse except profit reduce taxes on wealthy corporations close loopholes 10billions more to trillions…more corps do well gifted pittance to workers doing badly how much the middle balance medicare social security…'

'Is all we all want!' she yelled over the droning of speakers voices. It did not seem too bad, or even unusual: different channels saying different propaganda propping daily sensation to steer the minds of all those displace misplace misleading what is left-out not what is right-on: *the Television Experts and announcers liked to make a big deal out of anything* She thought: *it was their jobs after all.* The pictures shifted to City Office-Buildings. Steeled glass to the very Sky! that only a few were being *allowed*-into and then to the squares and circus' around Town and City Centres. All over the globe, all the streets and roads and highways leading-there.

The TV reporter turned away from the camera, and let the scene, *somewhere else: could be anywhere else*, speak for itself. In the kitchen radio reports followed from the stock-markets around the world:

'Tokyo Nikkei Shanghai Shenzhen Hang Seng Bangkok: Dubai-Mumbai Delhi: Kolkata…Carib. Mexico-City…'

'Indonesia. Saudi-UAE: Israel and Egyptian Stock Exchanges import-from export-to RTS Moscow Deutche Frankfurt Cape Town London and Canada Stock: New York Wall Street and Rio from Singapore to Iran…'

'Busan to Rotterdam containers Trading-Ports for Coal-Gas Oil&Plastic-Money: Defensive-position(s) established:…' as she went to look for tea-bags. He got the cups out and put some bread under the grill to toast. As the cups were emptied and the door was opened to go out. The Stock-Market Reports were interrupted by the radio-announcer:

''We' have heard in the last few minutes that The International Conference of Governments and World Banks meeting in Geneva are to make statements, at midday mean-time, on the current state of financial affairs across the globe. The Cost of-Living Crisis' around the world…' They stopped and looked at each other as they heard the announcement:

'What will they come up with this time I wonder? She asked aloud to him and to the radio speaker, and as she went to the bathroom door:

'Come on you two!' to the children, and to him in the same breath:

'What time are you finishing today?'

'On Lates!' his reply; with a shrug, noticed, as she said:

'I'll have to clock off early then', and she thought *another opportunity to postbag me for the whole-sack but if school finishes before work what are we supposed to do?*

‘I’m taking them in, anyway!’ he called.

‘I know!’ she replied:

‘We’ll have to go to the Super-Market.’

‘Tonight?’ added knowingly: *a reluctant necessity when it came to it*:

‘Or tomorrow anyway.’ as she kissed him on the lips, quickly, tantalizingly, knowingly *this weekly and often daily shopping-trip is what they did all this for. Along with the mortgage-rent and love of their family and children* smiling he went out of the door, onto the communal hallway:

‘Another financial crisis!’ he called out to a passing neighbour walking ahead with more than a note of sarcasm which did not need any reply, other than a disinterested:

‘Is there?’

She went back inside the living room, and went to turn the television off, as the announcement of the impending declaration from government leaders and world banks were being repeated:

‘Won’t make any difference!’

She shouted over the noise of the television:

‘…never does!’

She left the-home soon afterwards.

3. He.

He took the stairs with the children, two-at-a-time one in a pushchair, the other just learning to walk, and they headed off together for The Corner Shop. Turning at the top of the road, pushing the baby buggy uphill, the as if unmade pavement now, in disrepair, showing the lack of maintenance through the good times, as well as the now financial recession, austere-times. Telling *The Walker* as He and She said to each other in jest (*the children laughed at that…*) but the one *no-longer holding-on to the child-buggy pushed-on* called-out to:

'Hold on to the buggy' *answering the constant questions*:

'What is this?' and:

'What is that?' *and having to say:*

'Be careful!' *every* second, and:

'Stop! making me have to say: 'Be Careful' every second!' and they giggling together, at what, he knew not what.

Not ever imagining a time when he and she would not be going to work and they to nursery and school; then keeping them until them keeping us *in Our-Dotage:* Going to pick up the fallen walking running-off child grabbing the perambulator again, and continued walking-on the pavement and at the road:

'Do Not Run! the walking child only hearing the last word as usual:

'Walk!' and wondering what all the shouting was about, and running:

'Stop! at the edge!' hearing all the words this time: *thoughtfully*:

'O.K?'

‘O.K.!’ trying out these new words heard from them and at school.

‘Stop!’ and stopping in the middle of the pedestrian pavement. To get collided into and rolling on the ground giggling *in the middle of the road?!* getting up and running-off laughing, looking backwards,

‘STOP!’

at the corner, turning into the next junction:

‘Stop! at the kerb!’ He catching up, pushing the pushchair ahead, the walker hanging-on, over the kerb and into the road. Looking both ways, and then both ways again. Then back again, one last way this time: *too quickly…going to Run!* the way the traffic was headed moving slowly one car at the head of the queue stopped, and a polite hand to let them across, to a wave returned.

Watching-out, for all three, he and they and to the oncoming traffic split by traffic lights commanding: *Stop, Start, or Pause…*to the other side safety to the other kerb:

‘Walk!’ The-Children chasing on ahead to The Corner Shop. The ‘*little-‘n*’ in the buggy trying to get out to follow, shouting, and pointing with one, then both index-fingers, toward the road:

‘Taxi!’ swivelling around almost falling-out. Pointing, ahead:

‘Bus!’ the other returning, giggling:

‘A. Bus!’ *correcting*, and then at they passed the Shop pleading verbally and non-verbally tugging and whining for sugary sweets:

‘Helicopter!’ *heat* camera-singing, and pointing and swivelling around again:

'The-Corner-Shop!' the other:

'Sweets!' *categorically* usually not until they came home from nursery and school. Even then only some days, and if they had been good at school or nursery. But always worth a try.... *pointing* jumping up-and-down, on the buggy the other *falling out*, buckles unbuckled, by the older one:

'As long as you behave yourselves today, and they're not too bad for your teeth, and you clean your teeth!' *they knew that giggling* all the more, at some reference only they knew the words, the noises, and the tone of voice, the bedtime:

'Clean your teeth! Properly!!' the older one repeated, and they went into more fits of giggles. Into the newsagent-come-grocers and confectionary shop, and sometime licensed off-licence. Where He, and She, and They stopped each morning, for bread, or a newspaper.

On the way to Nursery and School, when it was His turn to take-them in.

Always the possibility both mythical and real: of *sweets* as well.

As they crashed through the door the older one getting deliberately, or so it seemed in the way of the baby-buggy, asserting rights over the other smaller and weaker and *re-leased* both leaning to and at the:

NEWS FOOD&DRINK 24hr.

shop-counter not un-usually but always predictably in the morning rush *with so many other things to think about* the only thought unable to think about anything else: *Children, shopping tonight? Newspaper? Sweets?* The buggy almost tipped over in the raucous, the older one falling over the younger-one strapped in, strained at the straps, snapping painfully back. Letting out an ear-piercing yell. The Older-One: giggling at-what? until the younger lashed-*out as only younger siblings know how too* and the older one let out a *Yell!* then a *Scream!* apparently exaggerated explication of pain from both now and claims of *un-fairness!*

'Come-on you're the Older One, you should know better! Do you have to have to fight and argue over everything? No sweets!' and then he knew, as soon as He said that that he was A Beaten Man; not for the first time he
realised knowing: *would not win every-time...*

A yet louder exclamation set up. While the younger looking on in glee, quieted and puzzled, twisted turned looking upwards to *The-Father* for some re-solution to the questioning plea and fell out of the buggy un-buckled:

'Me a' well?'

Looking up from the floor, the older standing and going to stamp on the younger, smiling sweetly now, the other sprawled on the floor as if fooling felled:

'Smiling Assassin!' He called-out from the front of the shop, in reference to the Older-child and to The Shopkeeper who was stacking shelves from remaining stock. He, holding-up the regular National Newspaper, the Shopkeeper called:

'Markets' Blind-Assassin:' looking at the newspaper on the counter-pane:

'Another botched Act-of-State-supported banking'...'

'Fiscal-Terrorism! You may as well keep that...' to the loose change being handed over the counter:

'News freely advert-sponsored!' hearing, and not listened-to until later, scanning the newspaper headline:

the money left on the shop-counter chuckling when the realised remark got:

'No, I got it.' *minding*: The-Children who were not fighting but pretending to steal, sweets *not knowing any better yet* knowing better laughing, and looking obvious. The Shopkeeper bagged and handed over most of what it was they-wanted, pointed at with shrill voices, still:

'There you are, for later Your-Dads' charge changed!' the customary sweets as a gift now *in-change sometimes anyway* for a small-note passed across the counter the sweets from the-Shopkeeper to them, and then him, waiting:

'*K*eep sweets…for later.'

The Children looking pleased, and anxious also, that they too might have to '*K*eep sweets…for later.' with only the then conditional:

'And only if you are Good at School today.'

'All day!' they chanted together. The emotional and ethical merged-again into puzzlement bonbon change-back to the-Father patiently waiting to get-off to nursery-school and work.

Again, consternation, put-on, by the Older-Child, to the younger pouting, dropped lower-lip. Acting-out, pretending, face pulling. Puzzled-at and copied by the younger. Both suddenly *laughing* at this, and between *themselves*, at something they did not *really* know what it was *to be Good* or: *All-Day,* or how, or what it was, to *at-(t)a-in* this.

WF4.27.

4. The Banker and The Clerk.

The *investment* merchant-Banker sat-back, and glanced across at the *administrative* accounts' Clerk, sat in the opposite seat, fixed-table between. Travelling on this same-train same-time, same-carriage. For the-Clerk the *same*-seat, if that or any other was to be had amongst the everyday commuters seated *and a few standings…today usually crammed-in each weekday, early-morning* into The City.

For the-Banker, this day too-early for the usual-reservation. With, or today without, waiter-served breakfast or a free-morning newspaper only those freely given-away and piled-up in the station forecourt to be taken-away. That had to be paid-for anyway by publicising the latest model and version, and most *reasonably*-priced. Like copies of The Big Issue sold-on by Homeless-people in Metropolis' around the world: *no such thing as a free-lunch* the-Banker reasoned. First-Class: The Financial-Newspaper paid-for anyway by The Railway Company: Public-Private Infra-Structure: ticket-seated and breakfasted comfortably with:

The-*Financial Newspaper* at massively *dis-counted* market-rate cost-price *freely* as-advertising encouraging in-someway paid-for, and for: *returns…*

The-Newspaper could be easily afforded, anyway. Today's loss-leader tomorrow's winner paid-for upfront from the station-kiosk day upon day.

The Newspapers Corporate-Investment: at-least *knowingly borrowed-on: perma-Credit: Merit: Staff=Cost(s): paid-off and on continuing steady-sales to be recouped; shorted, daily, and long-term investment…*

Achieved…anyway…today The Newspaper not given-away with the exclusively extortionately and permissive over-priced pass this day into the City Stock-Exchanges and Financial-Markets' covering staff-costs' paper-bark and oily-inks magazine loaded as affecting the whole-wide World.

The Annual-Executive rail-ticket paid-for, whether used or-not.

This day the first train out and apparently all carriages only Standard-class available. A single First-Class carriage was filled-up quickly by anyone who had a ticket and *conceivably some who did-not:* there were no-tickets being checked or paid-for *apparently* the barriers left-open and inviting *allcomers.*

For the-Banker, for another-time that morning, something mildly, now-seconded, and *markedly* unusual. The earlier, when the radio alarm-clock had switched-on routinely with the early-morning fishing, farming, road, and rail reports.

Airline and shipping stoppages and delays, arrivals, and departures, and speculative *forecasts:* weather-reports, from around the world, local, and global, political-economic and Media-Mogul manipulating-news with the previous-nights' *closing* market-prices from around The World...

There had been developments overnight that needed attending-to.

From the emptying platform the-Banker and the-Clerk had boarded the train together more or less equal. The-Clerk with an *advertising* Free-Newspaper and headphones plugged-in to a mobile Media-Centre. The-Banker with a bought-copy of The *Financial-Newspaper* from the trains' limited half-
empty double-decker food and drinks re-freshments' trolley.

Having taken the first seat available in the nearest Standard-Class compartment, coupled with a foul-stench reeking drain-leaking latrine *literally* retching between the brown and grey-green patterned seats along the narrow aisle way the-Banker waving the newspaper ahead *as if to clear-the-air.*

Un-wavering when shunted across by the next-passenger in-line to the only *vacant* window-seat glanced across-to and sedentarily leaned-forward across the table between them and asked of the-Clerk already sat down-opposite:

'So, what do you make of it all then?' in the customary easy clear voice of one born with the interrogative confidence of swift appraisal.

As in-stantly as if mysteriously-*accusatory* as if with some felt need for *validation, valediction, justification, testimony, guilt?*

Even before any evidential fact, or fiction? With a self and other-deceiving finality, justifying with instant-conviction…*but of who? By whom?*

Despite the original opening-question, it seemed as if with no real right-of-reply.

The initial conversational-question asked as if *intended or not* to be replied-to or any other-mindedly *mitigating* circumstances or any-answer-at all particularly or generally, listened-to.

Or so the younger-Clerk surprised to be spoken-to then considered: *perhaps like a nurture-nature kind of thing? Possibly a-Plebeian enquiry? Selected-standard flagged with no-probation* the-Clerk decided: *more likely a command, to make something of IT and to-be-taken-notice-of.* Notice given-of anyway disregarding of the possibly-paranoid maniacal rhetorical-answer awaited or not, by either, or Both regardless of the-Other*: The subtler -Inquisitor? The Quicker to-the- Draw?*

The original-*recipient* by-assumption looking-up from a streaming mobile smart-phone camera and videogames-console:

USB-4slot-machine game: WarFair4 *downloading*... PER (personal electronic reader)/de-pocketed-*information*-recorded singularly removing the ear-phone microphone-socketed-lead off-line *searching* for the source of the *mildly-irritating openly questive-words' spoken* as directly-to, or so it seemed to the-Clerk, in almost immediate reply:

'I don't know what to make of all, what?' then:

'*Senseless.*' Spoken as to The-Banker as to The Newspaper headline shaken-out the whole carriage could now view. The-Banker sat-back purposefully, purportedly, and provocatively to-unfold *The Financial-Newspaper* with the headline outermost upper-most:

WORLD MARKETS IN TURMOIL!

and *seen* again ***that***-photograph taking up the whole of the rest of the *grey*-top printed front-page remaindered, pictured in the *mind*s' eye.

Now, turned inside-out and with a staring squeezed blink of the eyes, fumbled as if in a freak storm, a blown umbrella, quickly folded-away.

To the-Clerk hung-out to dry having seen earlier the front-page photograph and one-liner top headed: **WORLD MARKETS IN TURMOIL!** re-conceived on-line *connected*...down-loaded and *updating* second to second milli-second, minute-to-minute mobile-version *uploading* freely...with-advertising optional:

free2view choice fee-fleeing *skipping ad…verts…*

The-Clerk looking-down and into the same recently now newspaper concealed picture; and slowly re-storing from *browsing*-history as *acutely*-historically accurately as-depicted *we make our own her/historyies* thought as veritably verifiably un-faked up-dated un-tampered with: mobile cell-phone-photographed syndicated and World-Wide-Web: *network*ed-scene: as at the end of the previous day: the-City: Corporate-Stocks and Government-Bond markets as then as now: seen *news*-printed and pictured from the evening before: a *litter*-strewn liking-to old ticker-tape paraded across: The Trading-Room Floor…

Forsaken, and an *unforgiving*-bank blankly waiting-screen strap-line banded:

Markets Closed. Markets Closed. Markets Closed…

the single-slogan as about to go up or down was not possible to tell diagonally from one corner of the screen to the other perhaps *tangentially*-to slip-backwards flickering erratically across continuously stuttering…across perhaps another:

Markets Closed.

Only-slightly *blurred* from the-top aloft above, or below, the perfect the-*normal* mid-way seemingly *ideally*-positioned not at the-*extreme* outer-fielded or even ever truly evenly-*centred:* but as *inside-out* and now, as stilled as then, as now centrally fixed yet as if no-longer existent, as of now, as of then, then no-longer anymore unchanging ex-change rates ever more exchanged on auto until stopped *perfectly* still in its tracks *nowhere* at all except: now, there: only as stop-framed time-up: un-boldly *bleeped…*

Cinematographically stilled, to be recorded, and repeated any movement as any-moment only *(i)m-pendent*…in the-*cloud*…that bold bland statement *flickering* nonetheless-memorific ally *fuzzily* held in abeyance:

Markets-Closed...shimmering-pixelated grid-table mapping *diagrammatic*…a *flickering*…a coming-together.

As a vertiginous horizontally remote-geometrically sited as a new dawn held rising over the Worlds'-Edge The-Cityscape-*skyline*…*di-verting*…

>Banking-*details*…*scams threateningly un-throated undeclared-bribery and corruption fraud on consultancy-management directorial-loan transaction-cost contracts hostaged hi-jacking debt ransoming-deals projecting unfounded optimism other-wise keeping quiet: the-private/public purse tax-dodge key-service locked-in as if this would be enough to boost-real confidence on-fixed and unfixed burning-figures re-vealed violin-fiddle-d'dee*
scratching wildcat warning strike without collective bargaining or social-dialogue re-moved:

> Weaknesses:…

<*Strengths* and:… *sub-titling* screen-fantasy theme: *distinctive* emblematic-corporate-creations: *dis*-owning any *real*-identity or real-*personality* patched-together buffer-zone: video-text typeset: *cast*-role freely-played-*ambiguous*ly between Good and Evil. Between:

'O.K.?' and not *too*-bad.

'One -*price* and another,,,' and downright-*incorrectly* dis-honestly and non-rightly err-responsibly stealing-sealing:

The-Deal: Generic-key: *Designer*-rip-off: online: *dialectic dialogued rogued gone-silent pick-up the media-time…*

<Options: with-structure and *series* arcade-style *deviation* from the *normal… too* complex-to-control if-at-all cutting-edge cut:

'To: the-City:…'

'Cost of everything.'

'Price of everything.'

'Indifferent.'

'Unthink-able unsinkable: Land-Air Craft(ed.) Carrier. Technological and Fiscal ex-pan(s)(i)on Peoples as Vegetables-Fruiting Printing-Money…' screen-pixelated:

'Perhaps, bringing the-City down?'

'The-*Country*?'

'Their-Countryies?'

'Whole-Continent(s)…' amoeba bacteria cytoplasm lichen on the surface… into Space-*breathing Glacial seen be-low*:

'Frozen! Iced-up Market: Co-Lateral!! Being brought-down!!!'

Un-fazed un-frozen.

'Financial-Pricing System…'

'Monetarist: The-World!' *ethno*-linguistically gender and cultural ability *d-riven*:

'Corporate-Monopolyies'…'

'Known as: The-Government.'

'Merit-(o)Crass Class…'

'Hardly. Us! Plut(0)cracies'…Dictatorship! Of: The Plebian-Proletariat ***e***-radicating common-Poverty…Eradicate the-Gentry!! Eat The Rich! Socialist-Dictatorship! Free-Trade&Fair: Social-Democracyies' Individualist Capitalist-Collective Communist-Wealth Gap-closed…'

'Sold-off.' *nonetheless…*

'Lock, Stock & Barrel.'

'Democracyies' Dictatorship of a Minority-Media Elite…claiming Oligarchial plane yacht ships everywhere en-forced first past the post dis-(pro)pelled pro-portional preferential: privilege… '

'To?'

'Port. Dock.'

'To pay and sell…not-pay again. Then?'

'There to stay. Familial. Monarchial. Dictatorship of the Worker Soviet-Military Bureaucrat-Bloc: China. 5G U.S. Eyes in the Sky. Smart-Plane(s)…Space. To: Live. Over-Everywhere. Solar-Wind. Across the Oceans'…'

'Buy-Out?'

'Good-tactics…'

'Global? Know of Any?'

'What?'

‘Tactics? Civilization? Rule of Law?’#

‘Democracyies’…’

‘Authoritarian.’

‘A good idea…’

‘But…’

‘But what? Free-Trade Capital-Fixed Authorityies’ power-rules penaltyies’…’

‘Brought-down!’

‘Bought-up!’

‘Bought-out By?’

‘Who?’

‘Why?’

‘Population. Grotesque *Over*:(I)nvestment: GOB: (i)n:

< Commercial and Re-sidential: sold-as: Leisure-Property: Port-Folio (LPPF): Strategically *falsely* pro-moted media-meme voted…

>Dot-Comms’ Energyies’ destroying…

<Nuclear-Chemical radia(t)ion…

burning...

>Trade-War.

<Fair-Rules?

>Far? Traded. Until now…Land Fast-Food Forest-Funding destruction and re-building of Buildings’ mortgaged-backed lending…’ b*y incomprehensible debt-instrument…*

‘Lease-licence losing…The-Peoples' Patent: Our-Selves!’

<Governments' Sovereign-Presidential. Big-Business' Areas of Expertise Core in-Corporations' Trade-Wars Banks'-Credited! Pensions and In-Surance Funding-Investment…'

'Growth!'

'False. Fake-growth.'

'Greed…'

'Scientific In-difference.'

'Perhaps the-Price of Civilisation. Obey the rules…'

'Bringing in the goods…'

'A Greed. Changing the rules constantly…'

'Breaking…'

'Taken-out for virtually more-or-less. Buy-low. Sell-High: Of-course. Growth. Build-on…'

'Bought-Off.'

'Hostage to Fortune(s)…'

City-Skyline:

'Same as it's ever been. Irrefutable science. Economics shock-therapyies nationalist imperial mercantilism revolutionary social structural-change …'

'National-Charity!'

'Welfarist Infra-structure Government Big-Public Capital-Projects…bringing in the-Harvest…'

'Genetic. Familiyies. Or-*not*…Global-*failure:* Fear-0f. Nothing.'

'F. Off! Declaring: Price-War! Hiked Interest-Rate(s): for Currency-Exchange: Goods and Services: un-hitched un-hinged:

<Trade-Wars' *list…*

Colon(den)ial(i)sation *sceptical…seriously conscionable knowing-best everytime no-matter what…*

> Trade-War? Peace? U.N: USA: China: Russe-Euro:

<Crisis…Industrial

and Servicing: Health&Development Bank(s): Asia Africa and the southern Americas to Mexico-City. Asia-Europe: Educating-bias everywhere…

<Local-Global *failure* bailed-out: of the Money-*Banking* System this-time@Money-Go-Round fun(i)mation:

'Bubbles?'

'Media.'

'In-Bits.'

'Triplicate, now. Quadratic…'

'The Great Oceans! North-Sea! Arctic-Circle saw nothing like this!

'Antarctic: Gas and Oil Seas and Ocean(s)…'

'Plastic(s)' Pipeline: Whole-Villages disappearing Hydro-Global!'

'Of-Course! Metals and minerals from the poorest to the Richest listed-value back to the various-Elites' money peasant-food and gadgets cheaply made heavily over-priced innovation patent-profit to re-peat endlessly digital-value and cost: Stitching-up the Globe!'

'Making…'

'Fortunes!!!''

'How?'

'What?'

'How? Sweatshop sweaters. Trainers. Childrens' athletic shoe-school Cambodia Kymer-Rouge gun-running North-South East Bangla-Desh Pakistan-West…'

'Afghanistan and … '

'Africa?'

'Back to *there*?'

'Flooded-out forests drifted Rift where it all started. Now drought famine war as the food rich and powerful cling on and the poor revolt and more besides: UAE. Irani and Iraqi and Syrian Desserts' once Great Forests preserved as oil…'

'China to Canada and Chilean desert only and Caucasian-Mountains…Sahara untapped Polar to Equatorial rivering to the Planets'-tune roadways and railways underground and into the-Earth Oceanic-Desert Sand-Shale…POGS: PlasticOilGasSilicon Salt-Sand…'

'Iron-Steel Bronze and Concrete Cement-Pipeline(s): Broken-into: blown-up. Under-the-Seas and into Space! Carbon-fibre and Oxygen: Hydrogen and more besides….'

'Nitrates?'

'*Clean*-Water?'

'Monetised poisoned *Arsenic-Wells*' be-*moaned*...

'Peoples' President-Colonel killed familyies live-on…'

'Solar-Wind Hydro-Dam Digital: Macro-Economics for: Outright-Profit. Genetically modified seeds…'

'US?'

'Food.'

'Max. of: The Peoples' Authoritarian-Imperialist Minority-Dictatorship of the Propaganda-Media Elite: Worker-Military Businesses-Bureaucratic Officer-Corps Anti-Trust Monopolyies' every sector 5^6 including chance-choice Investment Merchant-Trade initial start-up banking-loans to the shops and into peoples' Homes4Government Nationalistic Exceptionalism Corporations (GNECs): Characteristic(s): New-Era: Global: ones' and two's…'

'Global Communism-Capitalism five and sixes…at sevens…now?'

'All-Sector Energy and Material Goods…'

'Trillions Stocked and Stored. Labour-Markets Bought and Sold. Fixed far-ahead: Registered-Bank(s): As Bonus on top paying no-Taxes. None-seen. Who pays Taxes? Government pockets Offshore Banking Business OBB) Share-Holders'…'

'From Stock-Holders. Peoples' Infra-Structure: *Trusted*-Customer Base. Base. Worker(s)-Peoples' Beneficent Practical: (*I*)n-vestment-Future(s): (B(I)F(s): P(*I*)S(s)(*i*)…Poor? Pension? In-surance. Savings? (*i*)nvestments?'

'Of course. All: HiStoryHerstory@Secured.'

'Cost?'

'Real? Cost…'

'Profit: at any Cost?'

‘Sub-scribed regular in-come barrelled.’

‘Un-secured?’

‘Se-cured Hotel-Hospital Privately-secretive private-ownership of the means-of-production Private-Property by Capital-Accumulation.’ Outside: *Cloudy*

‘Pissing-down!’

‘Crapping-away!’

‘Now? Scrapping? Or?’

‘Scraping-Taxes…’

‘If You're the-Revenue I don’t *owe*…’

‘Revenue? Police and Thieves!’

‘Where?’

‘Anywhere! No. Where. Lowest: poor and homeless…

<Sovereign-City:

>Nation: State:

‘Less. Bread-Riots…Low Social Mobility (LCM).’

‘As: against High Social Mobility?’

Coastal-Town(s): *piss*-poor: apart from: Tourism: Guide: Taxes and fund(i)ng(s): supports taken-away: online: Social-Structure: Austerity. Bubble-burst gave-up. All its’ gains tech. screen(s): Stocks and Shares. Anti-Trust Corporate-Monopoly. Al-*Trusting.* Other non-monopoly bought-out sell-off and monopoly take-over price-merger: Monopoly-©ap(i)ta(*i*)l of Government-Monopoly democracyies’ despite co-operation and competition-rules un-usual behaviour us(*e*)ual behave(e)iou® soon enough…

Quantity-costs price-profit margin. Bonded: Global GDP (Gross Domestic Product) Securities' Cyber-Security Section: Sanctioning-sanction(s)... *Busting-dow\n* back-door: Tech-Hostage. Front-Door: Presidential-Banker Lawyer-Arrest and ReTail Offices' Home-Builder re-lease and re-leased and arrested again for a very long time self im-posed exile at-home or abroad. Inside-Track Consultant Health&Safety Greedy-grabbing Robber-Barons' Gold&Golf all Corporate-Trade Government. Public/Private Business>Industries' Data-Sharing re-gulated crap: (e)Comms-*hacking Cyber-Viral attack:*

Impact-peaks de-pressing troughs' costs' rise and fall faster and slower re(per)spectively-on: Price-cost protection-Tariff(s): on imports from abroad un-equal(ed.)-out across different goods costs and Services' stronger and *weaker* revenue-growth, any growth, domestically, and abroad, gone too-far out.

Africa-digital Zimbabwe-express know-how no-how Zanz(i)bar knowhow and U-ganda skills to produce doctors and scientists teachers and social workers better employed up to now, abroad, sending money home bit b($U)y-bit.

Over- reliant on Foreign Capital: U.S. Dollar or Yuan: base currency: *rumbling*-Rubles Rupee's and Riyadh's know-how from all over corrupt deadly Empiric-Europe en-Slaving Slav. Egyptian-African Euro-Caste Chinese Indian Arabic Roman Anglo-English. French and Spanish and Portuguese as Dutch or lastly and most terrorisingly terrifyingly, perhaps, until the next Reign of Terror. The French Re-publican and Germanic Belgian Nazi Monastic Congo. The British Empire and Americas' Chinese Arabic and Hebrew. Latin, English, and

Urdu/Hindi. All: the same language now, interpreted differently every where every one as far as either of them or anyone on the train there, or anywhere-else knew as of: All: Business-Dealings: Commerce that evening an in-stant before re-paired:

'Put(s)?'

'Stayed?'

'Stooppped.'

Both now in the knowledge assumed of the other. Both assumingly knowingly, unknowingly, yet-as simply *pictorially*- imagining that morning the scene as unchanged from the night-time before.

Then, as now: inside the City Stock-Market Building heavy-teakwood mahogany doors, tightly-closed, hermetically hermeutic-ally sealed a normally *fluorescent* glow turned-off. Except for a single computer-screen presence, remaining-there:

Markets Closed

as if readied for all time, previously, for this day. As if this had never happened before. Yet, 'it' had happened before. From the evening-before, as in pointless pointed *dire*-warning: once installed, as if permanently equivocally, perhaps, warnings, automatically, not to be taken too-literally, ignored, or ind(e)finitely *normally* meaning: *before the cleaners had cleaned-up and some, but then, not-everyone-else had been cleaned-out.*

Before *nightlife* restaurant and television cabaret the latest news and sport, weather then repose-taken.

The *on*-message only that:

'The-Markets will be open again and sooner rather than later…'

'This-day?'

Both:

'As any other day. Business as Usual?' *taking-over* the competing computer-programmers' co-operatively collectively collaboratively *algorithmically* metering *as an un licensed taxi-cab carrying and insuring business-plans financially under-written and over-insured.*

Under-insured, over-written, or re-insured, or not-insured at all: looking out the window: violence-*suspected*…suspended the-thought:

'Different.'

'In-different. An Act of God!'

'The Markets on Easy Auto-Selling artificial-intel. A.I.?'

'I owe U?'

'AllOU! An Act of Us!' *pre-programmed virtual-win, lose, or draw, cancelled postponed, and re-negotiated the Animal-Urge to risk, to succeed expected everytime to eat and win or destroy through mistaken error...* disastrous: circumstances unfathomable into living-liv(ed.) obliteration, nevertheless, un-constrained. Imposing the investment and Merchant-Bankers' insuring not adequately en-suring the values of private-equity stock in Government and Peoples' currency-bonds individually personally *self*-owned by self and or

Other priced-out; cashed-out back borrowed on payday-*loan*...

Accountant-Clerks' s*avings*-account pension and insurance, and country *clear* profit-to Government-Taxes, paid-in or not. Un-employment in sickness or in health: Well-Fare Tax-Benefit or not.

'Well-Fare?'

'Well-Fair Abilityies' dis-ability illness payment as compensation or re-compense in sickness and in health.'

'Or: keep-working to death!'

'Or, not. Paid breaks taken: tea/toilet booked in-and-out…'

'As we shall most definitely be at the final end.' *Abroad. Suitcases full of cash it may as well be, except electronically and to-be taken-back with inward investment, repayment in compensation hitting-growth yet hardly covering the original computer-crime in sin in-bribes and back-handers' dodgy-deals reneged on millions of them, billions, trillions on fixed-rates' false-accounting cash-in-the-bank. Cash that stayed out-of-the-bank.* Gold and Gems. *Stayed-out.* Moved. *Ill-liquidated, stashed-away: un-available to-government or to the-People stolen-to: spend. Of the-Family-Business and as of small-Company-Name(s):* seen briefly as painted hoarding pasted on the side-of-buildings.

>Plastic-Palaces: Oily-Advertising *as along the embankment railway-track, alongside sidings and stations to be* > > >passed-through > > at high-speed non-stopping…

All else, stopped.

Closed, shrunk, and engulfed by-globular enlarged Corporations' advertising-hoardings for Banks' Currency Economic-Zone and Country-Town passed-through. High-Street: branches, shops and as autumn leaves currency-exchanges, as-*laundering twigged risked* domestic clearing-houses for returns, or no-return:

'By the end of *this*-day.'

'All-won or lost?'

'Banks? Shops. People…'

On screen:

<Purchasing: Power-struggle status: life is a struggle…every momentaryies' altering changing switching mill.(i)-seconds' first: Profile-profit to: Interest-Rates: list…

>Equity?'

'Stood-still…'

'Quits? 50/50%?'

'Who wins does not lose.'

'Who loses does not win.'

'Really?' *All investing higher-and-higher with insecure unsecured funds in stocks and insurances:*

(I)nter-bank loans re-insurances, and re-sales…within (closed-text) the listings…

Over and into… almost as suddenly as the whole front-page picture re-pasted into-memory…

For the-Clerk far from *assuaging* the culpability of the-other now exposed as the deplorably irresponsible and *reckless* lender. Not, as yet, wrecked-borrower, *wreaked* havoc-upon.

To the-Banker, the- Clerk cast now as the likely irresponsible, yet hapless helplessly indebted, no-deposit poor credit-*rating* history *first*-time *mortgage*d and-*possibly employee*. As in: *Bank-loaned as salaried, invested monthly paid-off to be paid-back payday pay-check paper-money on-screen-backed and banked:* The-Bankers' Newspaper front-page pictorial held-out taut-and-proud, as a flag of convenience.

Or as a *crumpled* bank-note opened to the light of day, as checking the veracity of f*oldin'* money: cash: *Bill-Fold Bank-Account* the Clerk knew and returned momentarily to the hand-held now re-opening news-*filtering* screen-news news-paper heard again as the rustling of dry-leaf *cadaver*.

'Plastic-Age Ex-e-cutive: Golden-Account Oil&Coal-Gas Plastic-Paying: over again…'

'Techno-Digital Geek-World: General Engineering & Electro-Knowledge:

(I)(n)formation: Outside the Train-Carriage: the weather not that inclement, or autumnal for the leaves to be springing rising from their branches; or be freely-falling as snow-covered as foraging nuts and berries, for the long cold winter.

The Newspaper turned crisply inside-out and halved-again…

Both to the same page *skim*-read by the-Clerk earlier: *pre-registered up-front...next page*…and as World-Wide-Web free and as-*expected* to-be paid-for not: -*freely-enabled* seen with advertisements, and scammed, both *skipped*…to:

The *(I)n-sider* Report:

As of today there is so much owed, by so many, that cannot start to be paid-out or paid-back this day, or the next. This morning the stock-markets are closed. Once more World-Trade has ground a halt. All Credit-Trading, has been suspended. The trading of stocks and shares in recent times has left prices at such all-time high-levels, that, overnight, have collapsed. We are yet again in the grip of the greatest global fiscal and financial- fiasco, the greatest-ever Economic-Crisis ever-again. Further-down:

This morning in Geneva there is to be an announcement of the International Conference on Monetary Compliance (ICMC). There is to be a declaration of economic policy and intent. This announcement is expected to stabilise major-global currencies and exchange-rates, at some mutually-agreed rate. To boost-confidence in the banking-system and in Global Fiscal-Policy and World-Trade. A shared protocol, at Midday, world mean-time today, by the International Date-Line will…

Then:

'There will be winners, and there will be-*losers*…' spoken out-loud. Looking-up The-Banker as from The-Clerks' *laid-back* attitude drawn from the impending appended silence.

The-Banker now self-imposed exile *imaged* point-of-view of the pictured *closed*-markets of: The-*Barrel:*

'The Photo: AKA: The-*Cage?*: *calculated*-risk? Join the-Game?'

'Game? Markets Closed?'

'No-*real*-risk…then? Limited-liabilityies…only the-details to be added…'

'Then?'

The-Banker, on mobile cellphone earpiece bartered furtively and openly and loudly and confidently as if now *confidentially* swapped hand-signals and *punched* the air *slapped both*-palms together:

'High-fives! We are in the tens…six…*seven*!'

'B*illions?* If you Will!' and holding a-hand over the heart openly-palmed, and as sat, bowed slightly winked, a single staring- eye, as stooped to conquer:

'Trillions, now…'

'Quadrillion?'

'Zillions.'

With *on-screen* confirmation…*re-directing…confirming*… password…and printed-off paper-copy waved frantically financial-agreement-stipulating:

'Only to be signed-off…' lifted from the floor brief-case revealed laptop lapped at reading-off as: The-Clerk now speaking:

'Billions of the-Peoples' assets signed-off? For every-One of US on this

Planet!'

'No! No-one-else but Us!'

'No-one else? But? Us? Paradise Forest-Fire Fighting. Ultra-Power: Corruption and Lies...'

'Plastic-oil re-dump(t)ion poll(u)(t)ion…Energy&Water-supplies cut-off.'

On-line: from: Colonial-Farm: Petty-Plantation: UnderGround-Railway and now Home own-owned at Home. The-Clerk continuing:

'The *Markets* are *Closed.*'

'*Deal(s)* to be added, then? Details? How many-*Trillions*-more? Before-what? All is Lost? De-*valued*? Bought-out. What? Sold-off?'

'That is the name of the Game. Selling-off?'

'Buying-up…to the *lowest* bidder(s):…'

'People bought-off…as Land. As property. Same. Difference…'

'To the-Buyer. Or to the-Seller?'

'Buyers' market? Seller?'

'Dealt-with.'

'Deals?'

'Done.' and with a nod, laterally entrusted, undisputed, and further endorsed over-*lengthy* client midday luncheon.

Tied-in: *gifting* as charity by guilt-association *expense*-account accounted-for and through *electronic*-signatory: *pass*-name and number and as a matter of public-record:

'Public-Record Details. No longer negotiable…'

'Always…'

'Now?'

'Or; ever-were?'

The-Banker:

'Then?'

Tapping keyboards:

'Then?'

Then:

'All to-be *ironed*-out today…by the all the-Clerks' of All the-Worlds' Works.'

'Home-Works.'

As if spoken be-fore, many-times, both.

Informa(t)-*kwiki*: transparent liquid-like, solicited. Solid as an assignment.

Scenario: Proposition. Projected, through the air *cloud*-like as before the-bell was rung for-departure. As a *warning* to anyone last-boarding the train doors closed the train-carriage sealed and seated *up-front* aside then:

'I don't know what to make of 'It'. *Yet*…' *pause*…pregnant.

Then The-Clerk bought the-*thought* snickered *slightingly* to-self, as if spoken to: self. Then: *that* sarcastic-*thought* or was it sardonic? outlined *out loud*:

'I'll *bet* we will find out soon-enough anyway, don't you?' sounded in-differently…differently as if someone-else had spoken the words instead.

As a *gauntlet-glove* thrown-down to be picked-up:

'O.K. If *that* is what you make out of it. A *bet*?'

'What *will* you make-out of it?' Only as instantly-*realised* now, and as at the time-of-speaking earlier; and that short-moment-later as spoken now intermittently irritatingly *intimating imitating* only-now at *the*-Gamble only *seemingly* committed-to. The *un-certainty* now at such a communally, yet privately, and now seemingly *shared*-venture. This seemingly reasonable or un-reasonable as yet un-priced, as yet only a *projected*-proposal. There would be a price; and a cost too:

'Parityies' Purchase-Price Initiative (PPPI) and re-sale onward: *that* is all you need to know'…*as yet an un-bidden offer in-prospect* the seemingly automatically-accepted *challenge* as-yet to be fully realised:

'O.K.' as well as the-other, each spoken now and heard, and now seen:

'No going-back now.'

Both now *considering* the import of these words, the more thoroughly, thoughtfully perhaps than said and heard initially; those out-spoken mere words as to the-*enterprising* enquiry, negotiation re-quiring further-reply? In-turns? Or not?

Now: the earlier previously *saved* in-memory and as the *first-respondent* again. The-Clerk ignoring the possibility again of turn-taking, with another supplementary, yet, elementary question:

'Why?'

'Why?'

'Who?'

'Is?'

‘What?' *Puzzlement* pre-dicated predicament: *seconded* now by both-speakers. Triplicated, as here *almost*-identically mindfully apart reflected against all others...on the train.

On the Train (i)n the Train-Carriage: *others*-visible and seeing, through adjoined metal and plastic cloth air-cooled compartment and as if no further-apart or closer-to or from each *other*'s-truth and in each-others' *minds*: and *all this meant? Exactly? And how soon? How soon, is now?*

How much is-enough? And: *How much is at stake here? Exactly?* as instantly both now regretting the opening-given to the exclusion of anyone-else in the rumbling bone-*rattling* carriage as both-enjoined as advertently as in-advertantly now in a two-way dialogue of which at that immediate-point there was *persisting* yet only limited dis-or mis(t)(y)(f)ying or any verifiable:

Group-Loop: dis-mis(s/*i)(n)formation…*

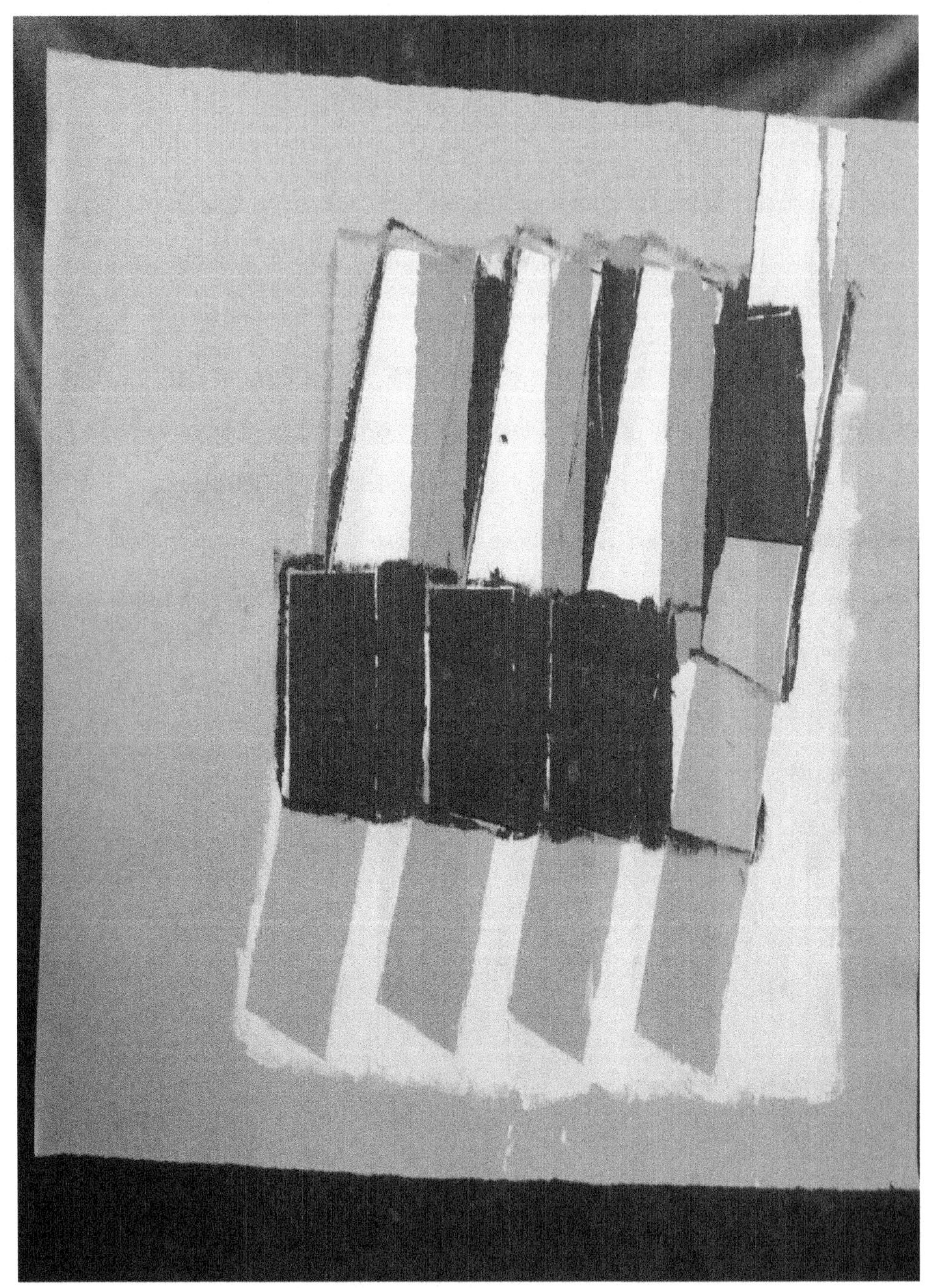

WF4.54.

5. The Accident & Emergency Department: Hospital and Home.

She had pressed the TVOFF switch, and they all had left for school and work. Closing all the windows and door behind her, a short while later and going where those others had left, and others were still leaving front doors for the days school and work, and activity ahead.

Outside and downstairs, through the piles of discarded rubbish and the door, wedged open to the blocked metal refuse-chute un-missed rubbish strewn everywhere. Pallets of *Re-Plastic* bottles and dish plates and bagging and carried to the blocked and disposed of.

The overspilling chute stacked with black grey and while bags on the stairs and the *If-it's-working* lift down to the ground floor: t*he worst thing standing inside the open lift-door not being sure if the elevator was going to work, or not.*

Or the elevator go crashing to the ground, like everything else.

He was *on-a-Late* and so *he was taking the children to school and nursery. She would be collecting them later today so* it seemed when her shift finished she could do overtime-hours or clock-off to collect them *if there were no emergencies that was.*

Then, either would have to phone one of the other mothers or fathers to collect *theirs*' as well *if they could...*

She entered the same **NEWS FOOD&DRINK 24hr.Shop** that He had recently departed with The Children only a few minutes earlier:

'Got any bread in?'

'You may as well take one there, only one-day-stale!', climbing-down off a stool-from-stacking-shelves:

'It's gone-stale already isn't it? Never mind the Bakery! Haven't seen them yet today!'

The Shop was open as usual ready to stock-up again with the usual days-supplies that had been phoned in the day before:

'It looks like it is: 'Whenever@The Delivery' turns up…'

Then, not for the first time:

'Your better-half works at The Bakery, doesn't He? They were here just a few seconds ago.'

Then:

'No sweets?'

'Maybe. My Other 'alf went out early today to The Cash and Carry, and not back yet. I phoned-in the order. They said: 'No-deliveries yet today! Nothings' moving yet…''

Then, in response to an expected un-expected received not ill-received:

'Still; there is Hope. I expect they've gone to see if they can get in the queue at the Cash'n'Carry pointing at the plastic damp going dry loaf on the shelf:

'Going stale yesterdays'…' momentarily paused, then:

'No-Cash! No-Carry!' *Exclaimed!*

'Fresh-is-Best.' concluded.

The Shopkeeper was stocking half-empty shelves the last stock sharing with anyone who came in the shop for whatever they could afford of their cash or card(s): Credit/Debit: continued to her as She looked at: The-Newspaper(s): on the counter:

''We' get from *Your*-Bakery you know?'

'Not mine, or ours, or even, we get nothing. Nothing. Cost of living…'

'For nothing@ItDoesn't last! Gets chucked away. Have to *Health and Safety* it or give it to *The Bin-Raiders* out the back.'

''They' have it? Still, can't blame them, can you?'

'Poor beggars. I leave it for those that take it. Homeless, you know, or out of work, on social welfare benefits that go nowhere, poor and hungry, *and* homeless…'

'That's where we'll all finish-up if we're not careful.'

'Easy done No-Job equals No-Home. No-Home equals No-Job.'

'No-Business.'

'No Waste mind. Zero-Waste. They take it home, you know, if they've got a home. Some have. Squatting maybe…no-heating they can't afford it. Toast it on one of those outdoors barbeque braziers. They sleep under the bridge arches, some of them, you know, no-trouble, except for the drinkers and junkies…out of it to get out of it.'

Continuing:

'Some have got homes 'though I don't know what state they're in. Don't seem to worry 'em! What have you got? All yesterday's fresh has gone. Panic buying!

Stock-piling. At the docks and ports according to T.V.:…' pointing to the corner of The Shop and on the wall and ceiling from where TV and CCTV *beamed*:

'Only that one loaf left now. Won't get another delivery today, I dare say. And I am told:

''We' don't know when!'

'Well, if they don't know when!'

Continuing:

'Only the 'papers delivered today so far and I haven't paid for them yet. I only get paid-for what I sell.' agreeably:

'Don't We All! Our-Labour!'

'How's that?!' doubly surprised at the apparent revelation: *that not everything had to be paid for up-front* The Shopkeeper came towards the counter of The Shop and continued chatting to Her:

'Business-Stock. All in *this*-Shop&Home. Trade-Credit Debt in The-Bank. Charge-Card? Not working…Banks switched 'em off. You can give me all the money you've got if you like. No change to give out 'though more sweets or crisps worth more than cash-change now:

'Chips?'

'Potato? Charge-Chip(s) OK!'

'Instead? Just like the last time!'

'Not-Just. All 'We' can-do.'

'And not-just like the last-time and time before that. No money in the Bank…no-food on the table.'

She exhorted:

'Your kids have got to have something to grow into…'

'Bankrupt! Not, yet…The Banks are not-open, so you won't be able to get any notes or cash-out anyway. Never be able to sell this place now. I've been trying to sell-off The-Shop and its stocks to pay-off loans and bills on The Shop *and* on the Stocks; but no buyers. I'd have to sell-off at too lower-price…'

'Negative-equityies' fixed.'

'My price too-high to what these Corrupt-Corruptors want to pay! Negative-Equityies and they know it, hold out until you cannot hold-out any longer, take the loss. I'll just up-and-go sometime, leave it all behind…'

'Lose-lose? Debt-Credit to who?'

'Geneology&Evolution…'

The Shopkeeper questioned:

'Same-Corrupters think they're doing GREAT! GREAT WHAT?! Not self-made like me and my familiyies'…'

'Inherited self-made morons! All respect to morons! Any buyers? For nothing@*nothing*.com?!'

'Less than Zero. Zilch. Sweet F'all?'

She asked in wonderment and not just *this Shop-Keeper. Empty-shop(s) all the local Shops were owned and known either by the name on the front of the shop and/or the Cultural-Ethnic-identity of the Family that owned or rented that shop its' stocks and shares and did their business their small retailers, family run businesses across the globe despite the Super-Market and Hyper-Mall still the way most-trade finishes-up from the home-farm roadside to docks and ports…in the air and to and from The Village, Town and The-City: Market-Places and Streets* and *of course, the wholesale-Industrial Stock-Markets and Money-Markets signage noticing:*

NEWS FOOD&DRINK 24hr.

24 hrs Open All Day.

She pondered. She looked at the front page of The Newspaper un-folded and thrown onto the *light worn* dark varnished and metal-trimmed wood shop counter-surface and service. She glanced at a cartoon which depicted the Worlds Finance Ministers: Politician Economist: *heads in hand s, sitting on stacks of money*; no words needed, but a comment. She read *for free* without intending to buy on:

Global Crisis-Meeting Midday Today!

The (*i*)nside Page:

In the last weeks and months there have been queues in shops for scarce goods, rationed by ability to pay, there have been queues to spend. Instead of investing against demands of pay-parity, pensions, and profits, before they became worthless. The prices of goods and services have increased week by week and day by day, as more Financial Insurance Compensation (FICC) Claims are made…

So, don't we just know it! So, what's so different! Or not! She *pondered* again. She wondered: *how the small shops and retailers and service providers like Health and Social Care (H&SC) whether large hospital or fast-food chain cottage-hospital or cottage loaf. How they managed at all? With all the out-of-*

town Shopping-Malls and Giant-Chain- Stores that everyone shopped at because they could afford the 2-4-1special-offers. The Scams! Price-up first then Prices lowered! Ha! When did that that ever happen without Prices going up first? Without any salaries and wages to give-out, what to spend on the Prices anyway? She answered her own-question: *The Supermarkets are paid up-front with loans withheld from suppliers until stocks are sent&sold cheaply from the farms out low-cost bidding each other and only what they thought they could sell at a good profit balanced only by what most-people could just a-bout (N/n)af-Fo(o)rd...earned.* The Shopkeeper had continued stock shelves without stopping hardly and stocking the shelves and aisle way cleared, finished:

'That's it! Everything is out. I'm now officially out of stock!'

'Preoperly closing now?'

'A-*part from what I've got in the back for me and the family for a few days...'* then:

'Packing-Up! Panic-Buying! and that's IT!' the train of *thought* returning to re-stacking the meagre shelves with the remaining stock and with some finality:

'Not getting in enough buying from the customers to cover the Household for a Day! Existing on Bank-Loans on Capital, Stock and Shop; rent is un-paid for the year. Tax un-paid...'#

'Unless PAYE (Pay As You Earn) taken at-source. Tax-Year: Governments Presidents' Sovereign Royal-Taxes! For *Our* own-good? For ***Their*** own-owned Goods only! Our-Taxes! For Our Own Good?'

'Theirs to get voted in again by fair means and foul Religious-Secular Monarch-Republican Presidential-Government Bank: Private-Wealth Equities? No. Ours. Enough-said.'

'They cannot give us our tax-money back so what, now? Fraud Tax-Benefits: For The-Rich! We poor to middling are the Majority! Of-course! Conned. All Piss-Poor low-paid workers now…if working at all! No paid tax-benefits! I Work long-hours…for this Bankrupt-Shop. Un-fair.'

She'd said:

'Fair? Just? Not.'

'So much more than only today…'

The Shop-keeper:

'Factory-Bread! Go-on, you may as well take it and yesterdays' News? Paper?!'

Then:

'Bring us some nice freshly baked bread to stock-up the Shop with from The-Factory as we call-it! That is where He works, it is isn't it? The-Bakery?'

She-looked up:

Then:

'They've closed the Bakery-Works, again. Credit-Loaf Crisis did you know, haha!:…'

'Import/Export: Super-Market Shop-Chains...'

'People as Things...'

She'd responded....

Then: The- Shopkeeper:

'There is a Rally at The Bakery, at Midday. Did you know? The Workers not allowed into the Bakery Works, closed, for Business. For anything! I owe them anyway. The Cash and Carry? You name it! I'm well into Negative-Equity now. The amount The-Shop owes is owed never Sell-Up now...Give-Way?!'

'Take-Away?' She'd said seek to cheer the Shopkeeper and Family now emerged from the back-room:

'Insurance Fire-Sale! Have to *give it away*! That is where He works 'though, isn't it? The Bakery?'

'Not any more it seems...' her *sullen* answer.

The Shop Keeper with re-newed finality:

'How about a *free*-Newspaper! Everything else has been taken from us, they've bled us dry!!' exclaimed, without irony; restrained and mixed with anxious *mirth:*

'That's not in the Newspaper...'

She said, to stem the merriment:

'Never is.' *Everyday Standard. Machiavelli-Metro! Sign '0' The Times. You know We can't even get retail-price4Fresh from the City-Bakery. News of The World paid-Newspapers...closing now. The-Others' for-Bad. For-Good. Just. Unfair. High Street Business and Council Tax and Rental Shopfront: for: Digital-Business: SuperMarket Hyper-Markets! Market-advancing share(s): %Chains Unbound Red-Queen Black-Knight White-Horses' horde...hoarding Atlas-*

shrugged Off-key: FountainHead@Ours! Our-share! Overshare: advertising: convertible: Space: Time: Mass&Momentum

Advert(i)sing: shared: Data and de-vices...un-regulated:

A-Gain! Re-gulating ourselves like everyone-else...every where: Social-Trustly no-Money! Low Wages and conditions of Work-Standards...

'The-Bakery...'

'*They*...*They* are *that* tight with their un-earned Profits' Gravy-Train for the Investors' not the-Workers Pensions&Insurances. Not-Us!'

'We have to buy our Daily Bread from the Cash&Carry too...'

The Shop-Keeper and She added together:

'Of course! How (I)dio-tic is that? Of-*Them*? Uncaring-for-Staff and Workers' Family! Domestic-Work at-home Unpaid!'

'The Bakery wants to make as much Profit out of All of Us as they can! Out of All of Us! Never mind the *measly* pay! Anyway...' and *pointing thumbs back through the door*:

'If The-Works are closed...'

'No bread and no cake either...'

'No Turnips! Not today, at least! Let them eat Turnips!'

The money for a small loaf was put on the counter and the large sliced loaf in its *mould-inducing plastic wrapper* and the newspaper with its banner headline declaring:

STOCK MARKETS IN CHAOS was carried off.

The Shopkeeper said:

'Take it...' and She took the newspaper, and left the shop.

She worked nights, evenings, day shifts. This week, this day, it was the late-day shift; or *the day late!* as some liked to call it. From the Ambulance-Station she arrived at slightly late and clocked-on. From where she drove the ambulance, maintenance engineer and assisted at accidents so-called First- Aider but not yet a Super-Medic like some of the other crews had a*ccident and emergency crew, trained-up in skills and procedures, assessment of injuries, life or death sometimes observing vital signs…moving patients safely, onto stretcher or aided walking. Checking for any changes to report to The Qualified Clinician taking relevant information, from carers and other careerists at the scene.*

Administering first-aid and emergency medical procedures, transporting people to and from hospital, accident and emergency, the elderly and frail to The-Hospital appointments. It could be anything: road accident, multiple severe injuries, or just a scratch. Taking notes for the medics, and the insurance, and police, if there had been A Criminal Act.

The-Ambulance at the scene-of-the-crime, alleged. Or the Fire-Service if there had been a fire, or if someone needed cutting out of a car. Rescuing, from a roof. You name it. Anything, and everything could happen, and did. Never a dull moment. A good job, a great job She enjoyed and was paid, well, reasonably well. Not poor. Definitely not rich! Could be a pedestrian, or housebound, head wound, heart attack, to broken toe. In a busy shopping centre, or on a country-lane. Sick baby and worried parent, or elderly infirm, worried well, or unconcerned brawler wanting to carry the wound back into the bar to show-off, not realising how much blood was being lost! That's when you needed back-up. Sometimes a suicide, murder. Under a train, them, bag them up and the undertakers take them away, to the morgue. May later just find out the official-cause-of-death: by 'crushing' or 'shattered' in the jargon. May have been pushed? On the roof, threatening to jump:

'Go on then!' *you always feel like saying:*

'...if you're going to! I've got children to collect from school!' but didn't: Once the Bouncy Castle is set up against the wall, and the suicide gets bored and tired, and decides to walk the stairs. Could be someone fallen down stairs. Beaten-up in their own home. Domestic violence, denying, screaming the odds.

Unruly, intractable recalcitrant, not well-behaved. Not well-mannered. Not biddable, broken bones, child-abuse, elder-abuse, anyone abuse, hate-crime or domestic public not funny. It would all be reported, had to be. To the Social Care Agent, The Housing Re-presentative...

The Police. They would press charges, if necessary Must do, ought to. Some of the things you see....pitch-up and patch-up and tell their story as well as our own: witness. Sometimes threatened as well. You had to stand your ground. Emergency blue-light, siren-wailing. Steering in and out of that traffic that never seemed to thin- out, or even give way sometimes.

Still, that was the job. Worth hanging onto.

Going-on to take the Medic and Paramedic exams, own time evenings and weekends, and bring-up the children! Check out the Ambulance. The-Vehicle: stocked with bandages, medical and life-support equipment. Ventilator and de—fibrilator fabrication *stored properly and in good working order. Comm.s equipment, to the control-room...*where she had started-out learning-how to differentiate one emergency from another.

Mobile radio-telephone video-link inside and out the vehicle, and The-Patients! *they would joke.*

Heckling themselves in their own pain and agony at what they had to deal with on a daily basis. All the abusive explosive exploitative 'isms thrown at them, but mainly anxious and kind smiles.

Then: *Checking mileage, speed, safety, on the road, and in situ...medical-clean.*

New documentation: date, time report charts, name... address if known, distinguishing features. *Check the fuel and oil and water, start-up, at the start, and end of each shift. Driving licence of course. Passenger Public Service classification. Different gross&weights and bearing, gear shifts and light and heavy goods for the larger vehicles used in public-(e)vents...* Now, 'though, the regular chat, only if there was time, stabilities' and solar-time time&energyies in the knowledge of how to save lives. When she got in this morning-shift the morning newspaper, with the Lotto numbers, and television and radio pages: *this job makes more than a TV drama any day of the week. Non-fiction* She liked maybe to *a murder, thriller or an auto-biography. Not many of them write their own, do they?* she thought to herself. *What next? I know? Nothing! Or the rest of my life! 'aven't lived it all, yet! Home. Children.* Hus-band...(ed.) The Accident&Emergency Room. Department and Hospital: corridor-wings were otherwise as *quiet* as usual first thing in the morning: *there's always time for things to change...*

'It always gets busy as soon as I think it's going to be a quiet day!' She called to a colleague, and thought to herself, *turn around and something happens, then it all starts happening! You hardly have time to think until the shift is ended, and no overtime-pay! When did I last finish on the dot, the bell!!?* she asked herself, rhetorically; and out loud to the others repeated:

'When did I last finish on the dot, the bell!!?' answering herself in response, with a thought-full then blank-*thought*:

'Never!' they all chanted as if they had done this routine before, as they had.

Waiting for the first call: that's when it always happened. Commuters driving from home, to work. A van, or lorry, at work, driven-recklessly. *Someone in a car crash. On the way to work, domestic, accident, or not. On your way to early-morning deliveries, or to a job late for. As if you are the only one of the roads. That does not have an appointment to reach. With fate, and a social duty ahead Slow Down! You are not the only one! Think: Safety-First!*

#1.*The-imperative to keep working too ridiculous time-set time-frame shifts.*

So, she could feed self and family; and others could be fed and stay alive. Referrals from night-doctors; there was always work waiting anyway. No later than sooner, the first call of the day. The druggies and the drunks, and the homeless who often slipped-in, and slept in the waiting rooms during the night shift, had been moved-on, for the day shift to start. It was not any different today, although the last call-out had been a disturbance at a local bank. Some missiles thrown and one person injured, the police were there. When the ambulance arrived, the crowd-had moved-away...

The-Other.

Ambulance-Crew and Nation-State Police as if they were guarding the money, not the people on stand-by had told them all about it, *the-incident, when they got back. The Bank had not opened. A queue, a line had formed outside many metres long and wide a gathering mobbing crowd really. Staff locked-out, and angry, upset, worried, scared some of them.*

Staff and Customer(s). With people trying to get wages and savings-out.

The Bank was closed, until further notice. There had been a scuffle between two of the waiting customers over an unpaid unwritten loan, and eventually, after others had got embroiled, two or three lay injured. Someone, bystander, onlooker, passer-by had called an ambulance. Several on-lookers came up to them, as they went to see to the injured customer, or patient-to-be; and the crowd, realising The Bank was not likely to open, had dispersed to await the further news; and to hopefully see if The Bank might open that afternoon.

She was on second call but was not needed. The injuries were only slight, but the scene was ominous, an omen it seemed for the day.

If real-disaster did strike she often thought *only enough bandages and food for a few days; and only if that is rationed from the start. Only enough food at Home, the same. The closer to The-Big-Shop time the less there was at Home…*

Go to the Local Shops when nothing-left-in-the 'House' as they called it: the Apartment-Home really, nothing left, at home. Not stocked-up recently and can hardly afford to go more than for a few days at a time, sometimes only one day, without replenishing need, and goods and services to meet those needs. Everyone was talking about the crash of the stock-markets and the announcement expected at midday:

'We'll have to go to the Super-Market tonight!' She had called after him as he had left; and She collecting the children later, after her first shift was done, on second shift later, split-shifts it would have to be. He going to Bakers' Work, *or the Rally, now? Collecting the Children?* Suddenly everything seemed more uncertain. And She really did start to wonder, what this day would bring.

He met a Work-Mate: He going towards The-Bakery or *The-Works* or The-Factory as it was known: The Bakery. From the Nursery School: passed The Old Church at the top of The High Road now The Local Council Buildings.

A Friend and a Neighbour from the same Housing-Block walking in the opposite direction, now shared the *journey*-Home past-by and from: The Bakery-Works Factory:

'No-good going-(i)(n) …' the other said:

'They've shut The-Factory again. Remember last time? Few more out of work, three-day week, again?'

'The last time and the time before that!'

'…and the time before that!'

''It's happened before!' was his blunt reply without irony, the Other replied:

'Closed down for good this time we reckon. Importing-bread! Do you believe that? The-Shop *(NEWS FOOD&DRINK 24hr.)* Shop-keeper said earlier today 'Prices-Up Again!'…*they* say…'

'Do *they*? Not Prices down then?'

'Never. There's a meeting midday…' the *Other* continued:

'Gates.'

'Factory-Fates! We'll find out then!' and laughing:

'See you there!' SHOUTed as they passed each other to their separate homes, laughing, at what, they could not be sure *like: The-Children*: waving and laughing too, at what, they knew not what; awaiting afternoon middayafternooneveningnight, when they may meet up again:

'Open for the Day!' *notice* pinned on the schoolgate re-passed, and now brought back to-mind*: Thank-Goodness!* had been the immediate response.

Although, there were mutterings and mumblings about whether The Teachers and Nursery-Nurses would actually see their pay and pensions this month or whether any of for how long The Parents would be able to keep-on paying-for the basic-education *nevermind the extra-trips and activities and equipment for this and that…*at least: *The School was open and The Children did not need collecting until She finished her first-shift and He finished his at The Bakery early-evening maybe, and she start her second-shift while he took on The Children again* then: ... *would the-rally would put pay to all their carefully laid plans for the day?*

-Will you be going into the Works?' texted when She had left the shop, and called his mobile cellphone; with photograph stored number gazed at but without answer, or voice-message reply and as he texted immediately back:

-No point going in before the Rally! Won't get paid anyway…

- What about The Rally?

- Going <u>Home</u> *first*… Catch the News…

-OK get bread OK? O&O 4now…'

'Don't forget after-school!' the Older-One had called after him.

'…half-day today!' the School-Teacher had joked and laughing together after sending a text about going to the rally, home, first. As the children walked, not ran toward the nursery doors, the school-doors, and He out through the school gate, he went towards The Factory Gates anyway and then after meeting The Friendly-Neighbour, they walked back towards their homes, passed by other shops, nodded and said:

'Hello.' to The-Shopkeepers and Customers standing around inside and outside, on the Street as they passed:

'What do you make of it then?'

'What am I going to make out of it then?!'

'Nothing!' he called back. Then to The Friendly Neighbour:

'Again.'

Then. He went up the stairs to the apartment balcony walkway. When he got indoors with the key, shouted:

'Hello!' only just out of habit, and switched on the T.V. again, and started to clear the breakfast things away. She had already set off for work with a sandwich, and the last of the bread, re-called calling afterwards after him and then he thinking: *did I say I'd bring some bread home? And* She said*:*

'I don't care if its stolen!' laughing:

'I'll bring some from the shop...'

'If they've got any!'

She said:

'Don't lose your job over a loaf of bread!'

Lucky, I got some in yesterday He thought and as if spoken outloud; *or sheer skill remembering what she'd told me before I went to work yesterday, and I didn't forget!* But this time…today… and as He settled-down, with a *last of the bread* toasted-dry sandwich in front of the television, to watch events unfold, he wondered: *or did I just imagine that? From some other time, yesterday? or at all, anyway...*

Anyway, what does it matter? We need bread, then, mindful *of the Midday Meeting at Work: and Shopping later at the Super-Market* wondering: *what would happen if there was no bread? No work? No money to pay for the bread, the shopping? The mortgage?* worrying reserving not for what would occur anyway, which as yet, he did not know for sure, for certain, no-one did, what would happen today.

Only what *might* may occur, could occur, which was all he could really think about. Home, and a sandwich with whatever is left in the bottom of the bread-bin.

Some *half-empty or half-full jar or a tub of something, and back to work* or Not *before the rally and the International-Meeting apparently at-midday,* anywhere reading quickly, scanning the front-page of the newspapers:

Stock-markets in Chaos!

Turbulence. G-Group Meet at 12.00 High-Noon!

CCClub in difficulties…

Insider Report

Today, there is so much owed by so many, that cannot even start to be paid-out, or will ever be paid-back. This morning the stock-markets are closed. Once more World Trade has ground a halt. All financial currency and credit/loans trading, the trading of stocks and shares that, in recent times has left prices at all high time levels, overnight, have collapsed. We are in the greatest fiscal and financial crisis ever; and yet *again…*

He sitting at-home *no- hurry* he re-alised, then, again, *if or if not before, this time: that He didn't have any cash. Only a couple of notes, the cash-card machines would be empty.*

If the Banks were closed.

There had been panic withdrawing, as well as buying yesterday, there would be risk going around and topping them up with new notes now, wouldn't there? Money riots? They will be headed-back or staying in base, with all the money! Armoured weaponized: Security-Vehicle bullet-proof dark and light brown, black and silver striped windows dusty dirt rumbling over the go slow cobbled pedestrianised High Street as if seen: shops either side, walking down The City-Centre.

Then. *as if (i)magined crowds emerged into the square and had emptied the Automatic-Teller Machine, well before, so simply locked, and empty. Social-Media connecting…*

SmartPhone(s) across-borders...Civil un-rest internally, toppling Nation-State(s) Shopping Trade-War rival(s): Knowledge un-missing transparency lies internet:

Techno-Chaos. Kaos, into a future of permanent chaos, for not slowing down but getting faster and faster speeds... Fake-New(s) Popular-arguing targeting-Military as well as Economic might:

Might may switch... to Cyber-Crime and Currenc(y)ies' Corporation(s) the size of any-Nation State-stationed *without borders frontiers of bodyies' brain-knowledge and hyper-knowledge of each in-dividual: Behavior-Data: as Universal as individually created emotional personality as UniqueSellingPoint Position(ed.): poison(ed.) umbrella and arrow tipped as hunting weapons factoryies everywhere...*

Now: Each of-us Cyber-Warrior(s): Move fast and break thing(s)…'

'Monetarise the-Data.'

'Data-Dream drive: eradicating deadly-mosquito: eliminating deadly-species…typ(e): otherwise: Owning Creative Common(s): No-Rule(s) except those made-up each time as we move-on to:…Networked Tech.(ed.):

'Not-fairing well…'

'Not-faring enough!'

'Not-faring at all!'

'Government-Co®p(s)(*e*): Nation(s)' State-owner: worker(s): Owned-People Free! Dismiss(s)-owned by dis-information: Safe-target(s)…
Chemical Crowd-Control patrol bombs barrelling through…

Demagogue President-Leader(s)' Sovereign-Game(s) of Throne(s): To-gether now....victim(s) of Economic Social-Change not perp.(s): Agen(cy.)t(s) with People(s)' signing-up: con.script(ed.) Authoritarian-Bureaucrac(y)ies with so-called evidence-bas(ed.) policymaking political shenanigans.'

'En-forcement of so-called Democractic-Populism…'

'Free and Fair: Geographic-Number(s): adding-up Minority: Family-Dictatorship: Majority minority of National-Elite(s): sameness born into Priv(ate)(i)le(d)ge®d minorityies…' dis-lodged…

'AllofUs! FAMILYIES' Peoples' Taxes: Business and Governance; Pay-Off: Premium-Freemium Benefit(s): Paid-for: up-grading: costume: Weapons and Loot-Box: People(s)' re-verting to type: violence…'

'Rioting…'

'Provoked attack!'

'At: The-Bank: Working-Labour Strike. Peaceful Re-fusal. Demon-strating…'

'Re-Venge of the God(s)!' Grand: Auto-Theft Rape! Pimp and Prostitute (*sshh…*) Not! Only in Military-War does the enemy Rape and Pillage!! Battle-Back! What-For? War? Fair? 4-what? By-Order! Trade-War(s): Of:-Leader(s)…'

On the field: back at the Centre:

'In the Market(s)…'

'Who have the Power to say No!'

'Power of Words.'

'War of Words. Legal. Too-much Power&Influence to deny patent-wavers acknowledge no-failure massed mobilization of numbers failing that shooters.'

'Vaccine-Money administered? Genetic…modifying service:…'

'Family Honour…Country…inoculation: Species unconditional!'

'To do nothing is to Honour nothing! All-Life! Crisis! Emergency-Power(s) of energy demanding protection…to not do something…selfish4thegoodofall.'

< Regulation propaganda known lies affecting morale heightened shattered re-stricting knowledge through science and religion(s)' re-viling re-generating con.spiracyies' failures every-moment: Elite-Tech.-Corp.(s).

>Government of People(s) of themsel(f)ves: Popular apparently as compromising enemies through quantified-Shopping and the qualified Ballot-Box: rigged-*fixing*...

< *H(*f)iring-democracyies' false-promise(s)' bought preferential non-proportionate:

'To: Day. As any day…'

'Nothing-certain…'

'No-guilt button.'

Innocent-E(v)so-lution: mining Silicon-Valley minorityies' of one Major-ally cost-free pricing Ads' Revenue: (*I*)ncentivizing: Popular: Competition-Wars monopolising Own Fam.-Farm Apple-soft cost-price

Consumer earn@Nothing! threatening

Trust-Foundation intimated-*stolen*

Benevolent-Capitalism

Democratic-Socialism

Commercial-seeding:…

Pay-Pals'in-debtitude un-healthy death genetic-Ally modifying re-putations…$Y(f)u0? Why? Best in the-Business strongest re-venue…'

'Rational-Kant! Imperative-Impeditive insurrectionist-violence…'

'That We possess….'

<No-losses@Gold-and-Silver…

>Analysis@Synthetic-Trade Power&Media:

in-fluenc(*e*)® mythical

Individual echo-chambers'

Gaming-monetizing money a-rising:

'Holy-rolling high-dice. No real-risk at all!' *blubbering-Whale Shark: intero-*

Gated:

'Over-sight re-view…'

'Collateral-Losses Non Re-View:' *oversight:*

'Tightly gripping experts' ex-pert…'

'Non-expert in: no-genius leader(s) minister(s) and excerciser(s): in the-

Knowledge@Analytic(s): arrogant-*shit* list(s): Game-Grift grafting onto trillionaire

causing-chaos mis-o®d(d)ering orders in ones' own image selfish work(oh)olic(k)

stolen money-addicted worked-hard no-fun…fun.' on-screen:

<Co-m(m)ercial: Musky Twatter 4twealthy dregging dragging (M)eta-Go(d)ogling Eco-Lab Uni-Technic Reliance-arty Halo-genic bit into commercial ad-vantage all be-cause they can.

>Producers of consumers' especially rich from the start made the calls' won-luckyies' un-lucky-lose some lucky-win some take-it anyway…from there *their* consumers as-if

under orders from: Colonisers' Imperial past Authorising-Regime Trooping-

Arm(y)ies' bureaucratically-tabbed stabbed-at: TheEnvy: The: TechnoPower of Money movements on-screen securityies' State-Police Esco(u)rt definitely and: The-Supermarket: *would not be open anyway since most people paid-by: Easy-Cash: Credit/debit plastic-card: Gold Silver and Platinum: Loyalty-Card: bleed into the-markets… the Staff dis-count: stocks of the stores: Goods in the Shop: River-Island and Oceanic Deep-Port dug-in:*

'Warehouses'…'

'War-Horses…'

There was shortage already on the shelves, after one day, yesterday.

The Bank Cash-Machines all virtually 24 hours anyway every day of the working and non-Working-week made-upto: $N/n...months and Years would go by like this. Then. It would all be gone. Robbed or hoarded possibly with violence with violent intent the Banks' they'll be closed waiting with stock guaranteed for the Prices…to: rise, again…

<Where? What? When? to rise?

>Or, to fall >.

'What?'

HeL/l...@Home ex-claimed to himself on-screen *image* of threatened looting hundreds and thousands of Shoppers *stripping the shelves of everything paying, or not.* Closed.

The-Supermarket: could be open for the next day; if everything was sorted-out by then He wondered *If? And how much would everything cost, once it was all sorted out? With what pay?*

None? Un-employed? Again? What about the food and everything?

Corporations and Governments duty bound to their Stock Holders, their-Voters; to put the prices-up to their customers? to keep prices down? Where? Trade-Wars? Price-Wars? C0st-price wars? Rich-Wars? Poor-Law Wars? Beggarman? Thief? Shopping: Pay-Wars anyway...

They at Home: would have enough to stock up once and then be broke again, and if we don't get paid into the Bank and to them, then what?! and suddenly he *thought* less calmly. He had to get some money from the bank and for the mortgage, had to be paid would the mortgage be paid? If The Bank was *closed*? *There was food in tins in the kitchen, and freezer and water in the tap. He had a little money, cash. She always had some...us(u)ally...so they should be alright for a few days. Perhaps? The Banks had been shut before:*

'Business-as-Usual! Bank Holiday! That's all. IT will get *sorted* out...' he exclaimed to himself and the Home. *Go to The Supermarket tomorrow, when The Banks would all no doubt be open again:*

'After all, *they* are not going to want to lose-Business?' he said out-loud and to himself:

'Bank-Business!' *i get paid so that they get paid and they pay people like me to pay The-prices' to: pay them back and so it goes around and no-one else there except the TV screen, on.* On the T.V. more reports from The Stock-Markets, around the world.

Those that had closed or opened and then closed, and not open for breakfast lunch or tea or dinner. The City, the Financial Quarters only, but not justly, waiting instruction from Big Business and Government; and The-Market(s).

Every millisecond of every day, everything moving, again. Experts, to give their Ex-pert opinion. Minor officials in the mix from banks and governments' made statements to the effect that The Banks were closed today. As if anyone did not know that by now. Unless they were brain- dead; or living in the middle of the jungle-woods, or the desert, or up a mountain with no electricity, no radio-frequencyies…original-wave tsunami of burning-bodies' *smoke-signal(s):*

'Bank-charges to be dropped to *minimal* and Taxes dropped too for the richest to stimulate the economies. All Worldwide. Government Officials are meeting to discuss the crisis.'

From the TV. The statement at midday would:

'Calm fears of looting…' *etc. never mind looting that had already happened, and was about to kick off again, somewhere, maybe even here.*

News continued to come in from around the world and was broadcast simultaneously raw and unedited reports on audio and video from Cities and Country-side.

Cataloguing the un-folding events.

The sound and pictures of people meeting being interviewed. Ready to comment on the announcements and their responses: at: The-International-Conference the most well-known and many totally unknown faces' exchange formalities. Beckoning each other forward, back or sideward, in gestures of Power-Broking and Politicking. *They* and as the audience were made to l*augh*, like *them* coyly, in public at comments made amongst each other shook hands and slapped backs. Press-conference and delegate meetings bull-dozed-in:

‘The Governments and Banks, however, cannot agree; either between themselves, or each other.’

‘What if they do not agree?’

Lines were drawn and withdrawn re-drawn and drawn, anew; still, there were too many *vested* interest(s): move the money around…

On screen:

‘That’s@)Sign(ed.) the agreement-document? Any0/Ones…

<Online: Global Basic Dividend/Ratio: NNN/nnn/…

‘Final?’

‘Was…not…’

‘Divide-again and-Rule…’

>Global-Basic salary…’

‘Insurance…’

‘Pension?’

‘Assurance?’

‘No.’

<Government: Pay-Bonds and Tax-Tarif(s) Session. Getting *re-solved…*’

‘Midday?’

From the TVRStudio: above and behind: The City: tarMacAdam: Concrete-Road Bridge and Railway-Junction. Various crossroads: TYXZ and T and X intersection forked, knifed and spooned: to The City seamless linked centre taped-off in yellow and black, blue and white, red and **black**, as a crime-scene, unknown-before. People coming into The City and towns, village-centre(s);

gathered, or emptied, travelling-out, and in. On MotorBike and Car. Coach and Container-Lorr(y)ies: like a crime scene; they were made out to be: common-Agr(i)culture eco-language from and to habitation Cit(i)zen as *d*en(izen:

-National-Exit: Securityies RE-Main:

-Presidential-Monarchial Famil(y)ie(s):

Union: Federat(ed.) Demonstrators and the Security Forces outside and inside CCTV cameras reached the Boardrooms and Bedrooms' showering informations leaking e-mails toxic enough, high-level: Puts and Calls being put-in drop-placed dropped/rose pre-©®ede(n)tial:

-On Present-Index: texting *sexting…un-moving…*

- Account: Credit: Default(s) Commission (ACDC) *(i)nterest*-rate(s): N/n: and Credit Re-bate A-bate(s): *altering*: re-payment:

Analysis-Scenario-1: News Broadcast:

''We' all seem to be holding Our Collective Breath; and await further announcement. People are arriving to work to join the meetings and demonstrations that were already gathering in great numbers at workplaces, town-square en-circling piazza and straight-honest and dis-honest street road in-and- out of:…

'City Centre(s): as The-Whole-World Protests in City and Town-Square…'

'What do you make of it now, there, then?'

The Presidents' Face appeared. It was difficult to tell if at the beginning or end or an almost endless sounding speech, *perhaps on loop:* The-President looked drawn, but was:

'Adam-*ant* no-changes would be-made.' after the *previous*-offer re-fused: of limited change had been ignored and *the speech went on and on round and round.* Reports and interviews, speeches, and the chants of gathering crowds. The claims of Government-Officials, Politicians and Market Ex-perts at Home and Abroad. Supplanted by de-clarations from people on: The-Ground. From Workplace Meetings and City Centre *Assemblies* and from World-Wide Web-bed: InterNet and TeleVision NetWorks: (*i*)n some places there was the sound of Police and Ambulance and Fire Sirens, the rumble of tanks and of truncheons beating on protective shields.

'On-line and in front of *your*-TV Stations…'

On the TV screens. On the rapidly re-booted: snarling-Smart:

Cell-Phone: *add-on* screens the picture *froze* the phone-book emptied:

Error message 303: *Invalid connection…connection closed…* as overcrossing an Estuary bridge unnoticed perhaps by anyone-else in the carriage.

In-difference if noticed or-not by anyone *else* at-all.

Except now each by the in-*Thrall*. Both likewise momentarily inadvertently, and actually advertorial making eye-contact: *flash*-framed each-other, and through the shared-window as in bright-rainbow and blue sky-coloured mirror imaged as through each of-themselves. Each-Other en-raptured recklessly, perhaps, or to be wrecked.

As if replicated, refreshing…*relishing* as then focused-away both to the outside-world as indifferently, similarly, un-differently, perhaps; yet *in-evitably all-ways* differently…through another Estuary-Town Bridge stopped for shunting. Freight-Train many miles long.

The #One back towards other-#0ne now staring and beyond both towards the as yet unseen, rapidly oncoming-*City* horizontally, and vertically to the same outside-world moved-past *moving*-past, and through oppositely; and thus as in-evitably differently *viewed* as to what was initially referred to, that too, was soon made *obvious*:

'Un-charted territory…'

'New?'

'(I(N)(n)ovation that is what is needed.'

'Staples?'

'Doesn't much matter *what* It is. As long as It sells.'

'Civil-Law. New-functions…'

'New-markets…'

'Broken.'

'There are the previously *drowned*-out. Fell! Through-the-roof!'

'Hung from the-Bridge?'

'Mental! Metal. And Oil and Gas and Minerals…'

'Plastics. If You can *get away* with It!'

'The same!'

'Oligarch(y). Again.' *crafted* legend on-screen: *names* and places times and as *in*-stantaneously:

‘Ungreen-wash mud-sliding and earth-quaking…shaking bursting volcanic *red- flaming…livid*:

‘Differentially Meteoric!’ collisioning colliding folding downwards, and inward full-fell yellow-brown red-and-blue gender unconscious-bias…

‘Holy-scamming…’

‘Stoning!’

Livid:

‘Once-lived! Lived-again! Solutioning! Experimental! Always Innovation! That’s what make it *exciting*…Even. Financially re-warding…’

‘Or-not?’

‘Forgotten. Fore-closed. Avoided. Evicted. Abandoned…

Squatted:…

‘Each season brings…’

‘New things. Experimental as in…’

‘Fashion? Scientific?’

‘An Act of Trust! Proprietary propertyies…’

‘Trusted-Trade. Analytic-Synthetics’ Ethic(s) Functional-*formatic* on-line: Political-Bureaucratic…’

‘Shock-Therapies’ tight monetary-military brute-force policies imbalanced Fixed-fight disappearances deaths’ work-eth(n)ic.’

‘Balanced taxes as investment re-moved…’

‘Protection. So, what? Who wins? ‘We’ do? Win-Win! Free-Trade! The Richest World-Business Politician leaders’…’

‘No-Fare shares. Somewhere-else: Theft. Looting…Greedy, then? Usury Zero-Rate(s): Social-Interest…parityies’…’

‘In-secure securityies?’

‘Fair? Where?’

‘So, who is not…’

‘Just?’

‘Exactly. Is not-*normal*…’

‘What is-*normal*, eh? Just? Fair? Normal? Parityies’ Se-Curit(y)ies: Lifestyle? You? Company: *Plant*? Eh? Journ(0)list? Keeping the Company-Line?’

‘I was here first before you sat down…’

‘But how would I know? Government-Officer? That’s ‘It’ isn’t it? Doing the-Governments’ *dirty* work?’

‘No.’

‘Digging-Hole(s).’

‘To fall-in?’

‘And filling ‘em in again…’

‘Going-to the Poles!’

‘Down? Or Up?’

‘You? Reverend-Revenue Regulation?’

‘With: The-Peoples Work in the…’

‘Tax-Office? Government-corridors? Room(s). Got the ear? Pigs' ear?’

‘Sow-sows’ ears?’

‘The Tax-Purse?’

'The *purse-strings* you mean?'

'In a barrel of our-own making…' each e-stock and commodity Government-

Government Bonded Share-Price passed each sell-by date out-dated: as lower and lower price-marker losses moved across:

A-Bridge: advertising electronic-boards against rows of banked fan-tail desktop screen(s)-closing: *listing*: achronycal and apocryphal-foreign and un-pronounceable or home-grown and *familiar*, closed.

6. Home

The-Clerk asking now:

'So. How did 'We' get into this *mess*?'

'What mess?'

'This cycle of in-debtedness? Again? This dis-*array?*!' into the screen:

'Fast-Action…'

'Slow- Mo(t)ion…

'Saw It-coming?'

'Pile-up. Hit the buffers. Off-the-rails…'

'Car-Crash!'

'Train-wreck? This *little*-Turbulence…' the-Banker perhaps un-expectedly uncompromising in: re-sponse, to the-Clerks' questioning, reckoning:

'Wrecking-Ball!!' *banging both closed-fists together.*

Recovering, The-Banker:

'There is a Market-Situation known as Demand-and-Supply.'

‘Where if a company doesn't have enough shares in stock to distribute and sell.’

‘Then this increases the price for these as a result: This is known as a Bull-Market…’

‘And this is what we have?'

'Or perhaps had…Bear Market?’

‘Or perhaps a Dragon-Market now?’

‘Eagle.’

‘Shark. #-Anyway…’

‘Whaling…’

‘Tiger-Market?'

'A growling Jaguar squawking screeching-Macaw-Monkey Market if you like! A Liger! A Tion! A Lie. *grrrr*! Bonfire of the Vanities! Acceptance, only Natural. ‘It’ doesn't matter what you call 'It' The Bigger Picture (TBP)…’

‘Smaller Cake.’

Thinking outside the-box…

‘The-Cage!'

From apparently outside the carriage, momentarily looked blankly, thought and spoke, the Banker through the plexi-glass to the outside world:

'If you like. The…*reverse*-situation…’ looking away, and then back:

'What?’

‘Supply...then Demand?’

‘Demand…then Supply...then Demand? Give and Take…’

‘Take then give…give…’ not getting the reverse-irony from the pen-ultimately simultaneously easy auto: *closing…*

'Un-concerned: Trade(s): anti-Trust: someone you know: Head of the Family at HQ. Trust-Buster(s): a-long way behind the-curve:

<Con.-sum(m)er-Welfare: Warfare?

Over: A-Bridge: un-named…*continuing* out the other end of a concrete cement volcanic: mountain-tunnel: subway sub-station airshaft: con-dit(ch.)(i®o(w)n)ing:

'A *Bear*-Market: this is when there is an increase in sellers…'

'I know *that*…and a fall in buyers:…'

'For: Shares: (i)nvestment(s):'

'Stocks?'

'Stopped. Goods: Services and: The money…*mostly*...'

'Cash?'

'Whose?'

'Toxic? Yours?'

'Mine?'

Bluntly:

'Every-Bodies'…' *savings pensions and insurance: investment: salaries and wage-rate(s): monthly... weekly and short-day: rates: NNN/nnn/...*

'This is now what we now have. Risk. Shared: The International-Banks and Economic-Zones: Government and Corporation(s): IT is a Global Market Shared.'

'Now the bottom has fallen out of it?'

'No. Share the Pain? No.'

From the-Banker, a printed-card handed over with writing seen:

The Rational Equitable:

Economic. Effective. Efficient.

(City Slicker Skyline Logo)

Nothing-else: black-leather cold-coated diamonte cream-cloth shirted City-spectrum blue-*grey stripe slick-suited:*

'Valuable-Equitable determined speculation on Equityies' Assets?'

'You think *this* is *Easy* too?' as if practiced before.

The-Clerk taking and reading the-*card* noted:

>Rational-Valuable Market(s)-Values' N/nnn…

<Logistics. Import/Export:

Then:

'Boom!'

'Bang-Again!'

'Bang!!'

'And ***Bust*!'**

'Again!'

'Stopped.' Then:

'Prices?'

<Fixed-Failure. Tax-Sub-sid(y)(s) or Sanc-Tion(s): Scarcity. Class-Interest profiting by starvation SubPrime: Mort-Gages' Homeless negative-equityies'…

'Space-Rocket Debt(s)!'

'Then?'

'No-Debt(s) as such, you see? You? Owing?'

'No. Debts…'

'Familyies? Tax?'

'Of course, they would not be debts otherwise. Pay As You Earn (PAYE)? Or not? Then paid in advance 1-3 month deal(s): short-growing season…1-3 years…then.'

'Research&Development.'

'What?'

'Don't know yet. Longer…innovation lead-in time and costs…' *spiralling…*

>Base Metals and Pharma-Food Mineral(s):

<Tech.-Priced: Valued: 3-5year(s):

'Harvest-Moon Money…'

>Taxation the same. In-Flation balloon bubbles de-Valueing: currency against other: Rich/poor list(s):…

>Subsid(y)ie(s): worth less/more to they who give re-(e)Valuating: reverse:…:

Imperial-Colonialism re-placement appropriation. Bought-Up See?

> <*Cheaply0(I*ES) falling-in…gradually:…

<De-b(t)it: Cre-dit: *driven*…investment…'

'Given re-mit: hit, hard, tortured, for *failing…*'

'On-(I)nterest made: Reason-able. Re-Paid. Credit-Debit: Paid again, see?'

'And The Cash-Funds?'

'Of-course, to draw-back-on...'

Free-running now on all cylinders The-Banker let loose, re-covering, on the tracks, next-steps:

>Stolen. Unfair unjust...

<The Stock-Market Prices bid with Power&In-fluence

exclusive.

Although always at some point in the past minimal seconded in seconds inclusive...

'pica-Quantum seconds!'

'Like last-night?'

'Confidence remains-high...'

'Others'? collapsed completely.'

'As the others...'

'Short! Risen by more than they are worth! Buy them up?'

'You got IT!'

'No, you got it...'

'Money?'

'Nothing...' *as the previous evening passed into-night and into this day* for The-Banker:

'From: First-impact Trading instantly as a Body:' *collapsed.* In the moment *between* open and closed:

'Fortunes re-tained...'

'And fortunes lost...'

'Not this one!' *in that brief second-take before the closure the final roll-call of coins landing face-or tail-up…*across the-Globe without the *liquid* monetary-assets to pay or re-pay; or, to cash-in:

'New: Target:'

'Space?'

'You Try It?'

'Go Up in a Rocket?'

'In case it blow-up you paid for it! For the *Asset(s)* to be burned-off!'

'*Asset? Whole-Corporation(s)' Countries' Land&Taxes:* Brought-down!'

'Safely. Presidents. Governments even! Greedier!'

'Gluttonous…'

'Rapacious.'

'To be sold-on…bad-pimped…'

'With non-*existent* Credit.'

'Just: on-paper:'

'Only. Un-Just(l)(y).'

On-screen:

'People-Paradox: Co-Operative-Competition:…'

'Author(y)ities: liars' paradox. Technical-offences small-minded simplicityies': Everything I say is False? True? Class-Corporate Rational-Equitable(s)? Reasonable? Just-Efficient? Economic-Financed. Effective? Finished? False-consciousness…other-Elite Class-Consciousness?'

On-screen:

<The Credit *is the Countryies'...gross!*

>*Gross Domestic Product over Impress-Port debt.*

'Where We Are!'

'All-Assets! Instant-Winnings!'

'Win-Win! All Put's made must Stay-on! Stalled!'

'n Stalled Precisely! Business as Usual! Trillionaires-Only!'

'Nothing. Is *moving...*'

As if behind a paper curtain hidden, heard, *anger*:

'Since the in-evitable: Pay-up-and Get-out.' the-Clerk now sub-claused:

The-Banker:

'Currency currently and con-currently worthless in name but shares worth the value of the product: Goods. Services. Not-making Primaries: but Secondary: Initial Re-Sources: Food and Water.'

'Shelter Work-Welter-Services Fire and Ambulance. Army/Police: Hospital and Social-Worker(s): Welfare Food-Bank. Re-volving Door(s). Security-HotSpot(s) Gangster-Gangs City-Civil Warfare. Safe?'

'Healthy?'

'Stock?'

'Money?'

'None.'

'Relative to others...not of-themselves *toxic...*'

'But *toxic* of whatever *noxious*-currency they are being bought and sold-for!'

'Exactly.'

'Or-*not*, as the case may be.'

'Nuclear!'

'Exactly!'

'Negotiable, shall we say?'

'And the-Goods?'

'The-property of whoever has bought or been sold-out.'

'As: moneyed-share(s) in the first place…'

'Except…now…Money. Locked-up. Worth no-thing. Stocks. Of: Goods on the other-hand.

'Good?'

'The-Actual. Got to get them-moving…soon.'

'And the only way to do that?'

Looking-out of the window. Across oil-field pipeline gravel graveyard pitted mined hillsides. Concrete cement-based conveyer-belt-brick-buildings, smoke-stacked flues…venting:

'With wider and wider differential-*ratings*…'

'Take a loss?'

'Only over last years profit-margin. No loss at all, then?' deliberately looking again, forward through the window, directing the gaze:

'Stalled-*also*.'

'Between one day and the-next…'

'Between one-place…

‘…and *an-other.*’

Looking, out-the-window:

'Until this Day.’

‘When the-*Bear* laid-down?’

‘Or clawed Its way back…'

'The Markets? Goosing! Taken to the air…or whatever….Crash landed!' and any other animal-analogy thought-of *statuesque yet misrepresented the otherwise rapidly turning-numbers turned-off, frozen and unrevealing shot-down drowned-out surfaced: exploded in slow-motion…in-pieces*:

'Shot-down!' market-marker board, and screen-seen pictured, mobile-camera photographed: on the train-travelling from where The Worlds’ Stock-Markets' early-day trading had or would have already begun. With the hammering of ancient cast-metal, a brazen-gong, heard.

A knotted-tied rope-pulled, a whistle or an air-horn, or an electronic *buzzer* air-vibration-*release*d…

Warning-signal…

‘Red-light…’ ***black*** as the night, yellow-red, to blue-green, as to the light of *day*.

As when the field or factory-hooter: blasted pale pastel-*yellow* rising over the horizon. As at the-beginning, and then again, the closing-of-Business-Trading. The-previous-day, where-ever it was; trading-constantly throughout the world, around the globe, and then as with each evening. following-on morning, to the final-days’ trade, and the next:

‘*Final*-Trade?’

'What?'

'Was it correct? Or not?'

The-Clerk checking-accounts' screen: *clicking*:

<Accounts? *closing…instantly* closed-down…

>Credit? *Advanced?*

<Profit in… T1:T2…

>Entire History of The World: Louisiana LOOP-tank blasted into mud and rock swamp…

<Granite and Sand: pottery

>Salt Iron Steel and Home.

'Still got a Home Public: Limited-*Liability* Computer-Company: or Glass?'

The-Banker:

'Aces-in-their-Places!'

'Done-deal bonus. Lucky-Money back?'

'Commission?'

'Profit-margins n/N…'

rapidly typing numbers and entering the fray…

'Building-Risk: Bonus! Stays! Stay-Put.'

'Until they are Put.'

'Again?'

'All *that* is in the-*Future…*'

'Exactly.'

'Now.'

‘So, it doesn’t *matter*, now?’

‘Ker-ching! Blinging!' behind the scenes. Future stabilizing then immediately:

‘Back onto the Dealing-room floor leveraging core-competencies…'

'Play for-today?'

'Pay for today!’

‘Daily-Me.’

Social-Media...Ticket-*takeover:* Boom! *waved* through…

‘Ex-hort and Con-Tort…’

Legal-Frame (e)(n)(g)u L-F (ING):

Border(s) uncertain: commission: fees and *fortune*: all: shopping-list(s): mis-leading data not-open leading data-*rushing*...

No-Going Back (NGB)

Federal-Trade Commission: Department(s): of Justice (DoJs)’ tax-cutting de-regulating trade-off pay-off post-Industrial off-shore natural land food social eco-environmental rationalisation of series of choices through de-ranged authoritarian hero-worship enabling accommodation compromised self-career serving…

The-Train: *re*-freshment(s)-trolley. Bought and Sold. Hot and cold, coffee and tea, and snacks delivered paid-for placed onto: The-Table: between:

'Well. Here’s the Deal…’un-questioning *intention* anymore:

'Further-loans at fixed-assured rates…’

‘Assured. To re-finance the debt.'

'What debt? You don’t exist without debt.’

‘Without Re-Venue(s): payment(s) made in data: puta(t)ive-takeover(s): Land Bank and Industry: flex(i)ble: FTC and DOJ. Your debt: cover possible-losses…’

‘Surely?'

'Re-Insurance bundled. Compensation-cover…'

'Bungled.’

‘Others? Guaranteed?’

'Never.’

‘Never use that word!’

‘What ‘never’?’

‘’Guaranteed’’ Personal-Bank. Life? Private Investements’ (i)nterest-rate(s):…felled payments increased with surety of: Inter-Bank (IB) Inter-Governmental (IG): Loans. Happens all the time. Self-Shareholder paying-fraud Rate-fixing…’

‘Price-Fixing? Cartel? The International Conference?’

‘World-Bank(s). Of course! Currency! *Electric*! Fixed-Price(s) Interest and Ex-change Rates (FPIERs) will take care of that! A declaration expected today. Midday…’

'Or thereabouts…’

Re-called. Stepped-back, looked. Stepped-up…and *in* again:

'No-*longer* Banking…anywhere?’

‘Yes. I know that! The Conference: To stabilize: Major Global-Currenc(y)ies: against each-other: Exchange-Rates.’

‘I know *that* too!’

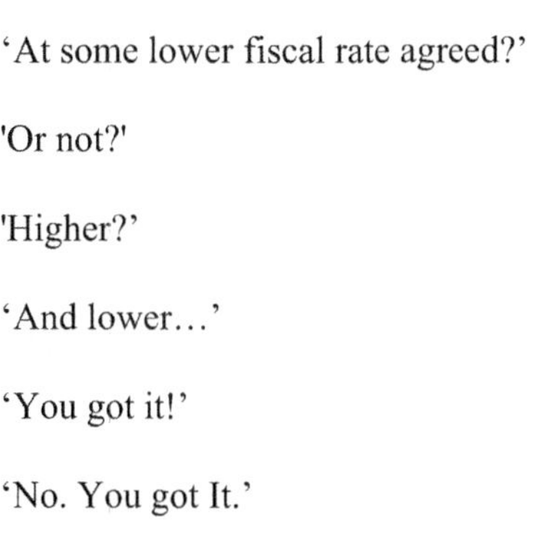

'At some lower fiscal rate agreed?'

'Or not?'

'Higher?'

'And lower…'

'You got it!'

'No. You got It.'

'At the same time:'

'If *You got it…They got you*. Public-Land Strategy Common Re-Source Re-Cycling What-if: The Inter-National Conference. Cannot agree?'

The-Banker looking-up sharply and out of the window as if there were nothing there. Where farms and factory-buildings, homes and retail-parks *flash*ed-by. Held. The-Clerk, as if sub-claused again, now. Left out-in-the-cold.

The- Sun: *warming* hillside outside, shouldered out of the window reflection…moving-on. Attempting, open-jawed to fill the *void*…but no words came out dry-mouthed, and with an intangible uncertainty, unfamiliar-*anxiety*, both, yet no so obviously one to the other, and again, anyway retorting to The-Bankers' incomplete statement, and asking again:

'Political-posturing Priorit(y)ies: Propert(y)ies. Building(s): Tech.: Money and Mond-Moral Benefit on the-line:

'And if they can-not agree?' *paused…*

'They can not dis-agree?'

'Interest-rates? Only? More…' *not even thought about*:

'Price justly-rises! Which they must Do! They will! *Their* will, of course, they must!'

'Otherwise?'

'Enormous-Clout! 'We' will prevail!' photo-shopped elastic-banded *sprung-back* missiles blasted into hordes of hired-mourners massed-crowds, gazing at a passing poster advert: both:

''We'?'

'Pay? Prices? Competitive proportionate-ratio's N/nnn…Stock-market…'

#'Stop-Market.'

'Super-Market…Hyper-Market(s):…'

'Securityies'…'

'Global-Government:'

'Armies' Army?'

'At points and places…'

'Bull: Bear-Eagle…'

'Drowned…'

'Dragon? Makes the-*odds*?'

'Does the Deals.'

'In money…'

'Some may-not return…' *everyday shopping? Going to the cinema, theatre…ever-again:*

'Bear-Cage.'

'Bull-fight.'

'Mexico-Eagle. Komodo-Dragon:' di-urnal solitary carnivorous hunters of PIG- and Dee(a)r-hunted Water-Buffalo Bi-son and *fishes* out of the house…'

'To eat?'

'In the soup? Some adapt.'

'Some do not. They starve.'

'Extinct. Fossil…there is The-Benefits System in Sovereign-Wealth: Fixed: to: advantage Who? Corporate-Government: Gamed. Personal-Relationships. Exceptionalism.' Bounced back and forth:

'Natural-Rights for Nature.'

'Rigged. And then it is over.'

'Then, there is the *mental* fight…'

'Real or imagined? Over, and over, in-*detail*!'

'A lie? *Changing* the-story…does not *Bear*-witness…'

'Ohhh Bullish!'

'Dragonic. Only the-*Truth*! Truth will prevail…'

'Eagle-Shark Justice: will-*prevail…' no-matter how un-likely driven, as being still, waiting for things to happen:*

Re-action. Response. Consequences. Re-(d)action. Unprepared. Prepared. Predictable: Un-predictable: scenario:

'Price-War. Shopping-Wars. Trade-War. Pay-War…Tax-War Benefit(s) Only!

Averting-*Disaster AD!:* that is what: The Conference: is All-about: creating the conditions for:…disaster. US *first…*'

'That is All!?'

'Ever-lasting…'

'*Everyday.*'

'Not today in both our favours, then?'

'Sure…

‘OK, so 50-50 then?’

‘Of: de-regulat(ed.) disaster?’

‘Or: of the profits…’

‘…and the losses?’

‘OK! Profit from Losses! You got It! P*atent(ly)*-Profit: DisMis(stolen) shop-thief marked-down Home-Stores’ Global-Stores available worldwide from *shared-* academy-styled: *re-search*: rig-fixed paid-for known ignored:

<Earth-Thief Big: Business: S*hare*-falled skyfalled per-sonal wealth fooled healthy un-health(y)…’

>No-longer rising…’ as unknown before…a-*moment*…then:

<Pay back-Time! @The Big-Banks: National and Private: Family-International: Global Co’s CEO: Limited-Liability Partnership(s): The-Government(s)’ The People in-Corporate.’ *in the background…foreground: pulling the strings…*

(Is) suing-suggestions: modeling modest debt-reminders…cash-flow cut-off threats if-necessary inter-cept interest *simple act of theft made complex in-law suit dismissed suspended hung out to dry sanctioned sentenced suspended….*

‘For-Fuel-flow cut-off…’

‘Un-necessary. Bargain: Trade-*Agreement*s: Trade-ins? For what?’

‘Farming-Subsidy…’

‘Pharming!’

‘Plastic-Money!’

‘Oil. Black-Gold.’

‘Local-innovation tax…’

'Call It what you will…'

'Ex-tracting: Cash.'

On: screen-seen:

'Deep-Mind. Deep-Water: Trouble…'

Nautilus-Minerals: gold, zinc and copper lustrous alloyed silicon metal(s):

'Making: thing(s) 3D – 4D. Metals? Minerals? Insider: Industrial: Digital-Machinery: made: Goods and Services: made-in: Internal-Market(s): Territorial-Water(s): slurrying slush silted: contractual-difficulties: MB…Holding Omani and MetalLionVest: Russia: Share(s)? Stock(s)? When? Highest-bidder?'

'Harvest Manufacturing Good(s) and Service(s): 'It' gets more-*serious:…'*

'News?' demonstrator(s):

'Stock-*broth* and Bread! Medical-supplies…'

'Could say that…'

'Armyies' forcing Trade-*stop*page?'

'Stopped?'

'Embargo-Sanctions stopped: re-started: food-shortages and no-water, how about that Siege-Currency: as Tra(i)n-Sanctions. Bite! Market? For what?'

'Currency?'

'Food.' *wet-and-dry*:

'Data! 'We' Grow Our Own! Stable *Healthy*-(E)conomyies'…'

'Whose?'

'Your(s): *Social-Stability…balanced…p*urely-Financial-agreements…'*on the sly sky-line glanced surreptitiously or* openly *simply un-challenged*:

'Balanced un-fair?'

'That is down to others' Politicians' People.'

‘Voters? Buy-Out? Or Sell-out? Buyers or Sellers’ Market Country4Free.

Communal. Army?’

‘Weaponseller?’

‘Depends, if you are a Buyer, or a Seller! Boom! **BOOM!!**’

‘…and **Bust**.’

'And **BOOM!!** Again!'

'Until it's time to go **Bust!** again…customer accustom(ed.) 'It’ is all about when you get-in and when your get-out…’ in the background now: *Car-engines racing against*:

‘Racing against Each-Other ignoring the-rest…’

‘Natural e-volutionaryies’ revolutionaryies’ selection…’

‘National-Selection! Elections? Express. Free-and-Fair? For later-Life: Health: and retirement from work for *Leisure-Time*@Re-search: development…de-signing titles’ run…’

Pixels’ pictured:

‘Push the Envelope?’

‘Whatever that means…what envelope? Whistle-blower blame-claim? Social-Care compensation promise never to pollute again?’

‘For-*eternity*?’

‘Family?’

‘Could be.’

‘Family-Farm or *Something*?’

‘Fam. Something.’ as a small-Business un-*flourishing*…m*ocking? Seriously*…Building-Site Tourist. The-Banker accordingly, affordably, breaking-out of the cyclical-contortion, if for nothing-else in-particular, except attempting-testily an explanation of:

'The customary re-normalising-writ to be re-presented.'

'Of what may be im-plied…'

'Not: in Real-terms: Economic-Ecologyies'… '

'Un-*Realistic*?'

'True?'

'Then…'

'You could say that. Monetary-Terms&Conditions: Business-Trade(s)-Union(s) *and that which will decide the*-Day….'

'This Day? Periodic-Existential-Crisis of Capitalism…'

'Nation-State Capital-Communism…'

'Radical-Democratic…'

'Socialist-Workers…'

'Monarchial-Imperialist.'

'Colonialist.'

'Peoples' Monopolyies' Capitalism.'

'Failure. Of: Collateral. National Investment-Banking Services (NIBS)' Goods *and* Services accounting-for:…'

'Raw-*material(s)*: Metals and *minerals from the Earth*!'

'GasOilPlastic (GOP)! Nuclear-Daily! Radiating Energyies' Treaty gain. Again! Land&Trade-Money It(s)elf!'

Pica-second by second...

''It' seems…'

''It' is only having *that* Competitive-edge.'

'Sales' Ad-Vantage…'

'Green-Elect/ric nomadic-gypsyies all of us natur(e) ally cultur(e)ally sustainable bio-diverse ourselves!'

Naturally?

'I see it in you! You're a Natural!' *a bit too sarcastically, or was it ironical, or even:*

'To be honest Anglo-Kings' Country Nation-(E)State. El-Presidente!'

'And otherwise?'

'RE-Public! Each President Generation: does its' best own owned lands sold-off. To stay-in for life. For deeds done…to stay alive…Good-enough?'

'City? Country? To be *honest…*'

'You mean you haven't been honest up 'til now?'

'Fair-enough. Too-honest, perhaps…'

'Who? All of us?'

'Or none. Everything I say is false…News?'

'You think?...True? Never mind.'

'Some…'

'Only if True?'

'Eh?'

'Only partly-true then partly-false outcomes…'

'If Tru(e)ly(i) (e)-Naturalised National-State lyin' and cheatin' im-position…'

‘Human Nature: *Animal-Spirits…*’ self-recognised...

Self-fulfilling in the glow of a *naturalistic*-fallaciously held-privately…and publicly-renewed self-*admiration*:

‘Laying-down the-laws. Voted-on Free-Will. ‘We’ prepare for 'It.’

‘’We’? Our-Will?’

‘Our integrityies’ here&now what of later? Trust? Friendly relative truths selective facts shifting sands who is the most convincing liar ’

Meeting head-on:

‘Economic-Diplomacyies’ scheduled-in on what? *C*ommodities. This Stock-Market…’

‘Peace&Prosperityies’ De-bacle! Do you? Or could you have been prepared for this?’

‘No. Only in the correct place, at the correct time, with the correct amount of *risk*-factor(ed.) as in: market-analysis…’

‘Preparations for a failed Harvest? Software-Crash? That’s it? Isn’t it?! Cover-up Cons’ piracy! You want Me to fix the-software Farm-Price. Pharma. Food—Price(s): M(ah)oney-Med.s: so-called tweek advertising innovation reviewed re-placed changed every eighteen months and going-down: N/n…’

‘Daily!’

‘Like the Hardware! Second-by second…faster and *faster*…no-one notices until the final second sales-pitch. Confidence in your product or not? What is that game you have there WarFare4?’

‘WarFair4. Only another Trading-Game: Energyies’ Cost-Price(s) War(s): Battles’ Bread&Bandages. Sold&Bought. Price(s):…’

‘Cost-Savings?’ *going-down…*

‘What costs? What savings?’

'Investment(s). Oh. The *Mighty*-Munitions' Malicious Malware WarFare? Takeover? Business in re-lentless pursuit of self-interest advertising enforcement through misinformation deception posturing immorally morally teaching our children to so do? It is the children who die, the old survive war, why is that?'

I kill myself

We dying from the inside-out

All my fears have pushed you out

Pushing you out never let the fear of striking-out

Keep you or me from the game.

Its' all I wanted and I get scared

I wished for things that I don't need

That I don't need all I wanted and what I chase won't set me free…

'Fraternal-FAMILYIES! Livelihood-Loans Home & the Credit-Debit Loyalty-Card(s): Mort-en-gaged Pay-Day Loan(s) (PDL): D*ebts* that go with pre-payment.

'So, You pre-pared? So, what are the rest of us supposed to prepare-for?' *to be starved into submission like subservient Pariahs' to be Homeless…and at War with the World. The Day the Markets Stood Still. Your-World@Peace roads walked natur-ally Easy. So, Mort-gagged. Credit/Debit card, or cards own anything else? Shop-cards? Loyalty-Card? How many Ex(e)cutive Or: non-executive?*

Ex-Executive? What about the Banks' Investment-Houses owned? I mean, owed? Shares: Pensions and In-surance(s): Re-in-surances? To: the highest-bidder. Get 'IT' now? Do…You? They own(err…ship) us People(s): Pensions and Insurances not: in-sured. Not pensioned-off paid-off for your silent-Ex-tortion Consumer Protection Bureau Circular-Power: Power&In-fluence to con-vince con-fidence chain exclusive-executive media-Power serving on the-Board: President CEO of Family Fun-Run Business-Board Family-Boss! They do as they please…

'They own Us.'

<They owe Us! on-screen:

>So. Down-to: Financial-Trust: again for Financial-Gain…

Number(s) on a screen: NNN/nnn/…

<Familyies' Banks Corporate-Government Mafia-Fiat…currencyies to:spend: on: goods product-sold over cost as ex-port over im-print im-port…

'They only want you to *owe*-them not: to: Own-Them.'

'Which We Do!'

'You-may do *might* with others' shares and insurances and pensions salaries and wages…'

'If-paid at all: Most of: The-Economyies' NNN/nnn…'

'Most the time relative peace and prospertyies' survival with fairtrade resource-sharing saving social heirarchyies' trade-offs…'

'Otherwise makes the news as poverty of war. Eco-Politics! *Relative* heirarchiyies'…'

'Social-domestic childcare eldercare ablecare unpaid.'

'Credit to them!'

'Owe-them own-them?'

'Familiyies'-Business? The-Big and little banks…'

'Corporation(s) Of Us?'

'Market-Floatation(s)?' *sinking…*

Global-Infrastructure Tsunami! Of course! The-Banks don't want you to own them. They want you to owe them Big-Time with interest-rates and Corporate-Authoritarian Regime: Climate-Crisis pro-test X-tin(ct)(ion) R…'

'Taxed to the hilt to pay for?'

'Police and Army Security:'

'Number(s) on a screen: The Super-Market(s)' sourcing-mistake(s) under-paying farmers over-charging customers not climate-change labour costs and protections failed failed failed…the Government(s) of The People(s) *the(y)* want you to continue *swimming* but not too quickly not too-much, growth, to start with: then in-finite…work work work…' *loading…load(ed.):*

'In a-*finite* World. Life…' *loading…*

'In: Finite World. This World, this Universe, Us? Continue paying-off whatever IT- is: new-Subscription regular *hidden*-payments:…'

'Family-Fraud For eternity! Never…ending.' *though(t-…*T…)

'Bail-out that is-all they want…'

'From? You? Me? Your Taxes, eh? Your Government?'

'Health&Education? Flat-screen TV? What about *that* gadget? Bought, or borrowed? Vehicle? Any other Property-Loans? Stocks&Shares' Insurance?'

'Stock-up, each week? Each month? Home? Bank? Starving-out Ghetto Slum-State re-fused re-Fugee Health and Social-Care Goods and Services…'

'That as well?'

'Super Hyper-G Lobal-Market(s) Traders&Traffickers! What do *You* want to b-*known for?'*

'Universal Credit-Card ad-vance?'

'What?'

'You owe *already…*'

'So, why not continue? EveryOne Does!'

'What?' *to any cross-trading traffic immediately curtailed blue-green cross-trades as another parallel and crossing-tracks passed and rattled and rolled-over like passenger and freight-lines. Passing like ships in the-perhaps moonlit-dark starlit night-passing that previous-night*:

'NNN/n. Margins-*called*: Magician's' call. Braking-point…'

'Br(e)aking-point?'

'Tipping-point…for-Climate?'

'*Profits: **NNN….***' and silenced skulked skull sulked sunken eyes and lights turned-out. Screen left-on, referenced:

'For: Life? *Markets'©losed?*

'For the Day.'

'Until: Midday.'

'Closed for Business.'

The-Clerk, to the-Banker:

'Final-Trade?'

'Close of Play?'

'Time to Pay…'

The-Clerk:

'Time to *Play*.'

The-Clerk moving around tapping toes and hand mumbling, to-self or to the screen-talking unawares, into the earpiece-microphone replaced-lead: *talking to someone? Talking to Who? Listening to what? Is that, singing-along? To what song?* Singing? Singeing-Singapore? Who? *Burning-WHO?*: Watching the-Game?

'Watching the-Game?'

'What-*Game?*'

Watched-in window-manifestation: manufactured: on-line *news*-updated…The-Banker puzzled at the-Clerk head-down no-further eye-balling body-contact and The-Banker *shuddered* at the *thought* of The-Clerk maybe getting a-head of the-*Game*:

'LoL'

'Ha-ha.'

'Got IT yet? You have got 'It.''

'What? The bail-ball?'

'The-outfield?'

'The Umpires' Whistle? Managing the Game?'

'Calling: Time. PuT-Staid? Stayed?'

'Time-0ut! Foul-Move! nn to NN Metre-line! Out-the-Park!'

Dropping-down, the eyes, leaned slightly forward, looking into keenly:

<Enquire-upon…@…from the *Market-place…*

>Pricing…guidance…mortgage/rent…pay…skills

<C.V.…fixed…fixing…overheads…

>Capital-amount:

Your-Balance-sheet: …

> >Credit…plus/*minus*…Debit…*indebted*…to: Bank of You: *opening…*

<Balance-Book. Capital-*Asset(s)*: list…*to sell-off...then*…to cover-confusion…

>Co-Lateral: owed amounts: to: *lists*…out-goings…*that must be-have paid…*

<Owned-Vertical?

>Owed-Horizontal?

>Owned-Horizontal.

<Owww!(ed.)

>By Who? When? Why?

>Up-and-Down. In&Out. Need-*cash*? because the-debt you *started-*with is the-one you're stuck-with: Life? <May as well be…*already worth more, or less than one-second ago…not only increasing the-debt…but decreasing the chances…of-recovery…as the-likelihood probability, of that-debt ever being paid-off…*

< IL-Logistic(s):Forcing your Currency to be de-valued:

>Which means?

<You get less-for-more: for-example: when you spend your currency abroad on-Your-*Imports* to *Your-*Country…then Your-*Exports* are priced-high to Others' Exports to You…as to *yourself* named: *list:* imports that you need, are expensive to you…

>Only what I need….

<Never mind the-*Luxuries*…

>You *can-afford them*…

<You need: *items: list…*

- *Bare-necessities of Life;*

<Your-Imports: Nn…pay-off…

>That You need to pay-off: Your Loans: list…and your…Bank-OverDraft: Debt: Salt-Mines: Cement-Sand: Securityies'…

BootCamp Cheer-Leading Masochist and Sadistic deaths: CoalGas/Oil:

N/nnn...and buying the things you need from abroad...not to save for future-generation green-wash deal only with the now unmindful:

<Expensive! NNN buy Status-goods' currencies *portable...*

>Anything...petrol-cars...TV LCD <

<Except your home... <

>Loaning money to buy with? <

<Those Corps shared in the Billions...

>Buy your bank and building society...

<Trillion(s): Now! Pensions e(n)surance <

> Loans to pay-off loans... < >Crashed. <

<Casino <

>Never. <

<Break the Bank then... < You either have trust or you do not

>Break the Trust...then... < I have had greater trust...faith unbelievable

Enemyies of the State action inconsequential a calling-card list of enemyies' State not of the-Nation but of the-self socially biased politically-motivated all:

<Mugged *then...* < in-quest...poison.

>That's about it... < self de-luded denial shaken irrelevant consequential-threat world-stage:

<Buying-out *other(s)*

> Sovereign-Currencies? Annexe-Axe surrounded-by protection-plot anti-career-corruption barbarism-medallion gifted...blank-taped material-evidence.

> Suicide-Selling? <Yes? <N0? <Buying-up stalled. Markets Closed.

>Cash-account...in the bank... <

<Uncashed…then uncacheable…

>The numbers stay the same… <

<The-?Value changed? <

>Why would I do that unless I was going on-holiday < Git IT in! On Holiday! >Health: employment based@:?

>Exports/Imports: n/N not-N/n… <

<Bonds?

>Travel(l(td.))er-cheques? <

>De-*values*…other <s against yours …N/nnn…printing more currency…quantifying N/n… <

<Giving-away Government Bonds <

>*Quantitively*-easing printing more-money… <actually pixels only <Inflationary? And *Devaluing*?! < seemingly-rich(errr…)!

<Buy-all privately-owned government-bonds/debts unde®-limited but for agreement for government to *write-off*...

>Debts: Nn…*default* with Dignity? <

<De-feat, with valour! <

>De-values yours against them…in monetary-terms… <

<So, the monetary value of the currency against? Others < currency… <

>Or <u>Currency</u>-zone? <

<Yes. Or Country-Zones…

>Caesars-Sovereign: National-Banks:…

<What isn't owed Caesar…

>Is owned by Caesar. What is Caesars' All: Presidents' Federal-re-*serves*…

< State: Reducing: N…n… <<Exports: for currency and the stuff currency buys…this is more-important than the actual goods < value of the goods… <

>Or the currency? *list…* <

<I want to trade for currency alone? <

>What do you want to trade-for-currency?

<Currency…

GoTo: …

<The-Bank <s: list: For Goods? Stocks?

>Servicing: National-Currency: *list...*

<Money? <

>To pay-off the debt, loan-credit… <

<On-paper? <*printing...*

>Feet of Clay… <No holds' barred…

>Lost to the World.

<Erin Callous…

>Jimmy. John and Bob 'Barclays' Diamond.

<Joe Dimon *character*: 'Temper in a Teapot!'

>Fort®ess: Balance-*sheet*:

<Valuka's Law.

>Arrows' Boomerangs!!!

<Angelo 'Countrywide' Mozillo. Meryl, Ken and Hank.

> Treasury-Secretariat:

< Troubled Assist Relief Programme:'

< Mortgage-Fraud! Inter-Bank(s)... < New: Sovereign-Presidential: >Start all over again! Like: Change-Trade: Saudi-Oil: OPEC Prices: N/n... >Bailout: For: Weapons of War. Food...munitions used-up as in-evitabilityies

Quick-aggressive move engine-e®ed through the-Kaos!

Rule-Random log *normal*-district retri-bution:

<Global Banking: Federal: Re-serves: bailing out the Bank(s)' Other: Fed. Re-serve@Presidents' CEO like lining their own owned-pockets...

>Fred the Shred!

<Gorilla-Office: >Guerrilla-Warfare!

On-screen: **The Country-Wide: National: Rational-Equitable**...

The Real-World: <Shares...*getting-there*...of the National wealth...*against*...

>*Super-subs*: Euro/Dollar/Yuan-*Mindi*...

<Sterling-*silver*:

#Gold-Rand/new-Ruble/new-Dinar/convertible:

<Peso's/ Rea and Rupee...: *forbearance* of your...Z:

'*Zombie*? Me?'

'*Servicing death*-debt:' *choking-off further lending be-heading clean-cut ripping out the guts in front of bogglingeyes: as they used to do:*

'Rubles and Rubel(s)!'

'No-Humility!'

'Humanity. *Bartering* Straight-Swaps. Settle a deal? OK.:...'

'Bartering Fair-Swaps!'

'Difference-debt? Interest only pertaining to profit…'

'That's how Bartering-Capital starts.'

'Cannot refuse food to the hungry homeless with nothing to swap…'

'So difference-debt have-nots to haves who cannot bear charity cannot bear to seem to lose! Cannot bear free-be kindness! Handouts only deserving praise payback for heaven not hell! Cannot bear others to succeed but be humbled by greatfullness! Altruism is Dead! Never was, was it? Always selfish other-submission always in humanityies' psyche? No need for need, for free exchange made equal by need. Needs be as needs must, for profit! Value of everything to self qualified as the-market! What Market? Yours, or mine. Ours? For Malnutrition Secular-Aid Christian-Charity Islamic Sikh benevolence Hindu Karma what else?'

'No charity or aid? Humanitarian. Give&Take. Take&Give. Supply&De-mand agreeably…'

'A-political. A-religious. A-Cultural Secular-Credit bartering value according to immediate individual need numerated…'

'Innumerate annumerated enumerate wants&wishes needs and emotional goods&luxuries…'

'Not government-corporate. Companyies' grant contract licence franchising price set by any arbitrary excessive tax-profit fixed in advance…'

'That you can get away with!'

'Begging?'

'Cartel-Negotiating every moment from making-stores to people…'

'Fakin'-Freeloader specifically quantifiable how?'

'Trust in God?'

'As we already have and see how that turns out!'

'Most the time O.K. OK?'

'&when it is not OK?'

'War. Trade-Wars...'

'Shopping Wars...'

'Currencyies' laws made-up and wars at the shop-counter...'

'Robberyies. Theft.'

'Bank-robber. Confidence trickstering trickling-down F-Theoryies' False theories' false theoryies...'

'Like this?'

'What? Who would deny the hungry food, the thirsty clean-water to drink and wash and a roof to live under?'

'Chosen for ourselves? Bartered for goodwill only? Why not? Property is

theft? Theft is property? Taking. Holding onto Doing. Exploiting that moment our own owned selves. Being exploited by authoritarian despot belligerent tyrannical...'

'Social re-lationships...'

'From the top! Un-elected Presidential price-per Mission. To be oppressed by others' propertyies' envyied envying. Powers' to control exploit appropriate appropriate common heritage of the many taken by the few! Self-made they say! To impress.'

'Only.'

'Familyies made like by us all!'

'To dominate-Dominion Empire-over Other: into *their* control without re-course armied and armed. Policed and police...'

'Excess profit! Can't help it. Buy-back cheap-shares excess cash-profit so purchase building construction-sites anything then buy-back your own shares! Makes sense doesn't it?

'Them Fruits of their Labourers' toil their inherited wealth to squander and afford to-lose! Always Win-win! So it *seems*...addictive...ignore the losses...of lives

'OnlineAuction-Barter Win-Wins partityies' fairness instead? Given ## Time to Trade ## doesn't lose...'

'Sometimes loses...not what you wanted or some info. gap so...'

'You can always pull-out...due-diligence...'

'Re-turn. From the-top, maybe. Never too big to fail.'

'Not a complete disaster. Learning experience...'

'Not to repeat endlessly because you can afford it! To: Lose®! You! Friends? say great! Personal-social value may go-up...'

'As well as down. You? Down today?'

'May change. The healthiest democracyies are those that do change...around proportional-choice...'

'The 5-3-1 choice consensus...no-one gets what they want all the time.'

''We' choose when, what, why?'

''We' don't always get what we definitely don't want either...Disaster like today!

'The Day the Markets finally collapsed!'

'Local-Global...*seeming*...'

'Give&Take?'

'Take&Give-back?'

'Hostile Taken-over freely almost. Wages&Salaries unpaid etc.'

'People. Propertized. Monetized...'

'Privatised A-Credit(ed.): Special particulars distinctive individual nature...'

'Ones'-own in-Societyies' owed credited owned to-live...'

>*Rates*-available: *list*...as above &/or-below *other*-short to: long-term de.-posits may be made...

<Life-Savings: Credit…in the-Bank to be: made…

- Quantitive-ease.

  - Debt-Lending-for *investment* at a *reasonable-*

    return…

  - or simply-fore-going…*feigning*…fore-

    closing…given…taken…back.

The Cash-Till: action-*armed*:

- Good-Goods. Local-Global items' little-*list*:… to-(s)pare

share-swap agreed and exchange for credits' difference not-debted from in-debted

if any goto: credited *save* same easier…as agreed:…' *click*...

'Going-down…'

'Sinking-Ships.'

'To get-Home: Solar battery-cell phone(s)' charging subject to ownership of land or goods…'

'Things…'

Qualityies&Quantityies: re-view sales' universal-credits internet of gadgeted re-corded shared give&take:

chafing cheap-fare bargaining haggling expected every moment credit-point scoring re-pute dis-pute cut strike stamp(ed.) attribute-to skill as tribute-to: sanityies' seeming proprietyies' non-proprietary excess ptoprietary superfluous counting-credit coin swap-same difference negotiate claim-courtesy in re-spect of bar-gainsale credit-price…

Each buying bought each selling-sold freely immediate near-future whole-future wants&needs…grasped enclosed within&without:

'Luxuries?'

'Pro-Parityies' Prosperityies4All!'

'Festering-federallityies' red-stone walls and grey-brick universities regional gifting…'

'Equanimityies' each privacyies' be-longings…'

'Owed-back for possession to move-in fairly deserted abandoned given-back.'

'Not owned…' good-fortune peered peers' examined weighted *propertyies' possessed…*

'Lived-in. Livid-on…'

The-Banker held onto the newspaper, brief-cased opened screen. Sat back, where had been leaning-forward in some kind of *reverie.*

Looked-over and stared the-Clerk directly in the eyes and between and around the other less-experienced in the ways of the world. Shiny-suited silver-grey not-dull-*charcoal.*

The Banker: a sharp-suited dull charcoal-grey power-dresser almost unnoticed rotund in-parts, like a tailors' dummy sharp-suited, three-dimensional 4G strung-out as a puppet *as to the Invisible-Puppeteer.* Staged-and sound-designed as-seen self-motivated moving synchronous photographic phonographic form…textured breathed-in…and breathed-out…flavoured movably moved: *recruited*:

>The Rational-Equitable: …

<Hostaged…*to fortune*…exchanged: …

>*Terror*-transformer: *with Fear and anger: revolt revulsion propelling political economic and media-pundit…*

<Expert-citizen…per-citizen…the-Clerk clicked looking-down not into anguish or fear but deprecation with de-preciation app.

>Basics-required…*restricted…*: *simplified independent advice-orphans charging model…specific one-off advice: inherit pension-portfolio managed-fees…*

<Fixed-retainer or percentage-fee? Y/N?

>Y…for *larger*-amounts…

<Less transaction-fee-deal…*through home and small-business and personal-credit*...on-screen bundled-up again: obliterating…un-traceable credit and… mortgage's and un-paid-loans…swapping. Loans/debts….send-to*: confidential.... done. delete...deleting...*

<Vehicle? List:…*chosen: V*8::Done.*

>Home? Furniture (including radio TV and all digital and analogue devises media and games:)? Food? Water? Air? *even?* Evenly spread? Across Your Life.

<Lives? How many do You *wish* to Buy? *list:* ...

>Every-one's-Lives?

<Only Yours…

>Selfish-Objectivism?

Does not-*compute: The Panic of 2001...2008...2016:* does…-not:Compute.…

<Objective-*selfishness*…

>Subjective un-selfishness…

<Un-Selfish…Subjectivism…

>Un-selfish-Objectivism…

computing all possibilities: now...chatbot: loving cajoling threat terrifying:

<The-Market: lists…of markets' *lists...*

> *Deleting...*

The-Banker taken a-back.

Beneath-what were actually Gold-Gilt Bold CAPITAL-type caption-topping, and a clearly no longer tumultuous Stock-Market re-called. The-Banker gradually and all too quickly, and suddenly and readily now recalling: implicitly getting-now, the pitiful irony of the newspaper headline:

WORLD MARKETS IN TURMOIL!

and the photograph below taken without permission, who would be-*have asked*? For: *permission*? To the-Banker, now again, forcibly revealed, for the first-time, by the-Clerk, perhaps, *notoriously*, not only into short-term memory but now also into open-consciousness sight as of vision:

<*Access Denied…*

'As of this morning...'

'Has already happened.'

'What's done is done.'

'IT is what it is.'

'The Worlds' Markets' un-*doing…*'

'Is what IT is.'

A-wakening as in a pent-up fury raging, invoked from the vestiges of the evening-prior:

'A phoenix, to rise out of the *ashes…*' *speech-bubbled spoken out loud?*

Trimmed-wings is what the-Clerk thought both saying:

'Business-as-usual?' both looking-out of the still-moving outside-window:

'Business-as-usual. 'There is to be a Declaration this morning…'

'By midday.'

'Inter-National Meantime…'

'This-will stabilise the-markets…'

'At some-lower-rate….'

'Others' auto-prag(m.)atically…'

'Higher?'

Lower-auto:

'And, and that is the-thing! What 'We' will do is simply re-align currencies….'

the-Clerk interrupted as if boring into the brain of the other.

As if to satisfy some lust or inbuilt hidden hatred unavoidable as both, even as

an idle-interlocutor:

''We' same-*thing*@50/50 Equity? Or at another relatively higher-point? Lesser? Or more? You got it!'

'No, you got it!'

'And start all-over again…'

'At: *some* lower-point?'

'You got it. You give me the-nod on prices of one thing and another and I will

do the rest, get me? Now then, those debts, who they with?'

'*Errr*, you?'

'O.K. Right here, right now' *as issuing some oratory declarative. Without clue of real-implication*:

'Like unusually *honest*-politicians yet unaware of their truth…'

'Only that made-up by themselves:…'

'All-Ways!'

As: (i)f there were such a thing as *honesty ready* to be barracked. Self-deprecating and yet, as anyone appreciating of themselves, deceiving of-themselves implied depreciation of the-other any other. With the opportunity presented, as an explanation of the rise to glorification yet also, thereby pre-emptive fall from grace all-be-it: if-only *temporarily:*

'Known Collateral-damage? Un-*intentional* consequences…as in current circum-stances as *currency-account…*'

as simplicity 'It'self and with which 'It', would all be re-solved today:

'Lawyer? Politician Soldier-Worker: F(a)m(i)l(y) Business-Banker?'

'Free-Trader Independent of course!'

'The warnings given taken?'

'Too-late. For that. Warnings un-heeded. Unstoppable! After the event…'

'…and hold *that* Front-Page!' that nevertheless now could only now be seen from the-Clerks' supposed, and *likely derisive, and probably gloating, satirical per-spective.*

On the side screen-panels rapidly absorbed concerning the latest sports and business-media Celebrity-Star: photo of stage and screen, religiously-inoculated to:

'Keep up with the-Markets!'

'Keep up with the…'

'Other.' *through violence theft on-TV Obesity meals fluffed, plucked, personal-value emotionally in-distress consumer-hazed blazing marketing-characteristics: Corporate-Crooks herding gentle-gentile rough-rogue as loan-sharks encircling the flotation-tank propitious-publicity canary in a cage. Down the mine. Mining-credits.*

A(g)gro-Credit.

Of the Media-photogenic

In-crowd the IT-crowd, and for the crowd of passengers generally-un-attainable.

Un-obtainable@ and therefore to be utterly-loathed, or loved, in equal unequal measure.

Perhaps, as well as envied for their art or wealth, or both, and thus taken a part-of: m*ost alarming of all the guileless, seemingly-misguided, business trusted-bought: # The-Newspaper-Owner: Media-Magnate.*

Now, the even more incongruously, and mischief-making paradox-inducing intent of a supposed-Ally.

Not-Enemy.

Anyway, not-yet, anyway: The Tycoon-proprietor. The media-Mogul Magnate-Oligarch empirical pseudo-psych-economist fine old art wheeler-dealer and owner with-whom…only maximizing

Profit-matters…

Golf and Gold may have been shared-interests and at least and

a singularly badly-shared literary-joke: this is not charity! Laughing together. Not laughing together.

'With Power&Influence…' *still marking cards, making-detergent soap or string-balls…*

Media-Empire: whatever it was it mattered not. Although 'It' did. Betrayer, betraying even spiteful little-threat, whenever not-making out. At the end of the day: when push-comes-to-shove, no-one is or ever was your-Ally. Not even, your friend, not even your-family. Bailed-out. Bailing-out from the false-accounting phone-tapping mass. Criminal Power-Corruption and Lies…simple rate-setting, premium payment protection racket-rocket.

Perhaps before anyone had tumbled...tumbled-in could have at least perhaps seen it coming. Could-have, perhaps should-have, acted with even-handed propriety, notoriety, *perhaps...'*

'Got away with Murder!'

'Suicidal!'

'Murderous.'

'At The End of The Day.'

'Criminalityies'...' accusation denied and replied in-kind unkind grin leer sneer simper-smirk...

Acting, sustained un-stained pure acting-for as if with assumed-impunity and as-usual uneven impropriety summonsed-up and convinced and therefore convicted in-their absence-of-wit...

The- Editorial Traitors! The Public: Closing-in. Closing-in...

'Closed-them down! I would!' *and closed-down the oily print-run down and*

deliberately stopped the newspaper and the train-company from delivering...

'For-Free!'

Then:

'No more Hand-Outs?!' *let slip:*

'No more Bail-outs Transport Coal-Gaz Oil-Wells Benefits who? Back-handers...can't get out easily once the paperwork is online coded passworded.

'Re-cycling...'

'Re-*purposing*?'

'By and for whom? Super-Power: Hotelier Medical-expenses School-College University abroad. Health, and Social-Communications...Media-Suppliers...and re-Tailors...Fashionista...'

##'The-Works...'

'The-Works? Supporting…'

'Denial. Confidence they are right and all other are left or wrong or all three…'

'The: Rational-Equitable.'

'Equitably rational?'

<Stocks&Shares…

>Store-Goods…

<Services…*financial* or:

>Free-Trade&Fair-Trade Food…

<Health and Social-Care Logistics…not:

>Wheat and Weapons *in silos and on runways out the window...*

<Civil-Protecting Military…*radio-equipment...opening…*

>AirCraft Carriers? Battleships? 'Planes? Tanks? Soldiers?

< *Non*-lethal…*supporting…*

>No-Other Fly-zone: destroying whole-armaments' *industries*…as

Boom&Bust leading-to catastrophe beyond any Command or Control: except

PLC Nation Inc.:

O Steam-Punk Investment Level(s):

<Complex: *connections…*

Connecting…*connected…*

<A formidable Labour-Union: Defence-Contractors…

>Aircraft-Tourism?

> Information Tech. Healthcaring Pharmaceuticals…

< Social-Care Home-ware…

> Premiere-Class. Business-Class Freight. Military? Family? Too?

To: Credit-Holiday! *Until things get back to normal, better, improve, not get any-worse...*

Both. One: not-connected…re-…connecting…disconnected…*re-directing...*

Desktop: *we are sorry that you are not-able to...your connection has not worked properly...*go- online to find a solution to this problem? y/n: OK? Y/N. *yes/no*?

<IN: Defense of Democracy: No? Losers…

>Authoritarian-asserted accomplice enabler…

< Protracted bloodshed certifying caucus democracy-succession trans-gression suppression…

>Yes! *we are sorry that you are not-able to...your connection has not worked properly...*go- online to fix this problem…fixing? *click.*

< Greedy-Gas Warships observed over wind-farm electricity supply North Sea North Atlantic World-Wide-Web cabling...

> Subterete suberate supress subterfuge marine in the skies...space...

< Potential sabotage espionage connectivity issues raised high-alert...

>Drone(s) Double-click…fixed: *fixing...*

< South-Sea Solar-*Soft Corporatism: never Powerful Struggle-Enough!!*

O Calibrating Competition Committee: Agenda: Monopsony: One-God Only Re-Publican President!

OSelect: God is within all of us…

O Power-gods each of us to win:

< Factional-Fruitcakes:…*fictional*…almost…

>*Excellent Executive-Foreign Mono(p)0Ly-Sony: Non-Executive director…*

<O*n: the Board of Director(s):…*

>*Presidential: Pro-tracted* Capital-Communal Infra-structure Building(s): Land and Food Machineryies' Trades and Craft Worker-Unions built by soft-souls and hard-hats.

<Value/Risk: N/n… deposit/investment covered.

>Utilizing-maximum…

<Capita-*profit: communal-paid engineering and on top of that: economic risk-cheated public-private infrastructure sharing between C2C (Country2Country) place and people to people populations proportions and actual-goods and buildings' routes and ways…*

- Visionary-failure: To establish perpetual-growth in-proportion to inheritance and wealth earned… *and taken:*

Industrial-Wage and Economic-Growth group-linked:

>Taxation and poor working conditions…

< Laboratory-tested Research and Design. Costs. Expenses. Price. Production…

- Promotion-Shopping: for: Amazing-Bargains: Amazon: E-Bay
- Ali-Baba Mittal Reuban Hinduja…
- TATA: Transporting concrete Iron-Steel safe-Homes cheap-Hotels bought-up…
- Manufacturing: Home: Health&Social-Care…

- Own-Owned Familyies'-Bank Geneva-London-Mumbai (*legal-dispute battle-skirmish proceedings…war in the courts…only…*)
- Bejing Fashion-bijou F&F 'family&friends' luxuryies' re-sorts…
- Bolt-Hole Armaments? > *protected?*
- TenCent? >TPC.
- 10%? WHat4?

<First-Step: Buy-cheap: as if poor: for: nothing: ex-changed for:

>Food. People are being fed false information(s)…

< Fast-Food. Not-starving…

> Fat-Food: City-Countryies' Epidemic: Glass-and-Steel.

<AT&T and IBM.

>Firearms&Frappuchino:…

<Change-for the better? >

> State: S(I)RCO.-Prisons meter-bids fail…

<We are: *Sorry …for selling-weapons of War?*

>For getting-*caught* others eventually all others scurrilously scarlessly blamed…if you don't look. If you don't watch-out others are coming to get you.

<Giving. Forg€tting? >Not Me!

< Check-it! >

>I will… >:

<They will be in-sured used *against…*

>Killing: *innocent(s):* Parents and Children: and *real*-Martyrs: Peoples' child-soldiers un-willing front-lines toted necessaryies for familyies' survival and peace.

<For themselves only led by others'

>Controlling and Commanding: Be-Sieged. Steel-girders, and glass and concrete: Dot Comms.' PharmaChem.istry and…

>*(E)lectronic(s):* The Future: *bringing out the past from sand and rock; water and wind and gas an oil: solar, wind and water (sww): every-home gain government corps swindlers no-longer excess-profit are part of the National-Green Infra-structure scheme many are well-ahead with: list:…*

<Trade-Peace! > What4?! <Fractious…*fixing the rates…* by *the Big-Six or whatever…*

> *Everywhere: homeless&poor….*

<Within and *without*: Civil-Government: Nation-State: %'s (i)dentical across Historical-Geograph(Y)(i(k)es)!

< State of the Nation! Nation of the State! *Everything-Else?Everything?*

>Every*thing across 91% time(s): surge-Price! Switch!!*

<Everyone… *>Everyone?!*

<Of course, so?

>Everyone else pays…

<A little-each…

>Makes…a lot of nothing. Advertising marketing public relations slipped-in fakery lies rubbish goods wasted management! At 0.001-0.2 actual of a *slight* billion trillion alteration upwards pressure on keyboard costs prices doubled tripled to account for inflations'…low-wage(s) long-hours…

<Gig for-War Jig!

- On The-Streets 'Own-Boss!'
- For-Wealth! Control for its own sake. Of its' own-stake in all-ggods available de-liveryied lied advert still stopped…
- Whatever cheat steal cynical con.fidence pyramid selling anything?

- Scam-Pride: in the excessive Profit not the Wares. Replacement goods continuously broken busted money-go-round never living up to the hype but the money comes rolling-in…

- Others' Health!

- Planetary!

- Global!!! Good4Life!

- Pragmatic-(*I*)deologue loses public again takes the wins craftilyies makes good…for better…older-other:

Ethno-linguistically gender and ability driven strategic-falsely *promoted tactics using-history*:

<*Clash-of-Civilization(s)!*

<Evil. vs. Good? >

>Good. vs. Evil? >

>Not-wanting to *Lose*: any of it! <On-*Fiscal*-Security?

>Pay less? Or? >

>More? Military-Security People! *Beat* them down! No-business operates on Real-Economy terms, you must know that? Rather on simply…

> Real-People: *unknown…pure*-monetary terms! Doesn't matter what investment is-on…for-profit. > Food?

>The-Banks?

< Shelter: *Real*-Estate: Markets NN/nano: >

>What >We > Will?! do…

<simply re-align currencies: list:… >

<Will >

< *We* >? >

In-contestably…

<Economic-Global: slowdown de-limiting-growth de-stabilising dam-aging re-stricting raw-materials pricing-out debt-burden (*e*)merging servicing suspending re-payment re-emerging global de-livery chains' supplying semi-conducting partners' shaky-sanctioning heightened geo-political tension costs' tightening monetary-policyies' necessary measures re-bounding waves' pan-demic flights' floating on choppy-seas seized re-surgence in-flated living-costs stable-demand leading-to: social un-rest galloping into Trade-War in-criminalisation-al…a.i.

>Stabilise the-Global-markets at some lower-point and carry-on:

<Pro-Market Initiative(s): Everything will start *moving*…

- 'You may have to fight a battle more than once before you win it.'
- ©onflict(s) of (I)nterest: Copywrite SI: significant-individual…
- Player(s): One Two Three… intra-vention:
- Inter-play…Atletico…City…
- Sports…culturally naturally evolving rules based adhered to in the re-public-realm:

< Refereed Trade-Constraint(s) (RTCs): re-(s)training simple screening process: limited and pre-dictable: as evidence: analysis-now! Future:

>Again. No longer Universal finger games, but on paper…

<Do you Buy or Sell? Simple…

>Stay or Put. Buy? I suppose?

<With what?

>Money!

<If you've got it!

>Eh? If you've got it?

<Flaunt-it!

>OstRich:' *head in the sand:*

<That is not-what I would do. I would watch the next one coming-along, the next one to grab at the opportunity: # scenario-2:

☢To knock-them-outa court! I have got it! Natural! >

<That is all it is. *Natural*? >Cheat >Ommisions…

<*Natural*? > Notional >Alright? Maybe you did not think President CEO-Banker: *acting in their own best self-interest* could be

so…so…

<So, mean? >

>So-selfish?

> >Think they Rule!

< Greedy! The-Law! Off-side! Lustily think they are the-Gods that made all the living-creatures… > <So un-caring! > Caring.

As if on *automatic*:

> Penaltyies' Scientific-Economic Game-(SEG)Theory *pish*! Push! Only following rational-equitable order >s? confusing contra-dictory > as dropping-*bomb* >on an unseen *civilian*-population…

Trickster-Tanked.

Looking into the screen hostaged as *distanced* from…the *thought*…the-pictures: destroyed ancient-ruins, bomb-crater homes: <So… Stupid! > confusing contradictory enemy-self: everyone-else: ordered:

>Damning Neo-Nazi Fascist-lies… >

<Part Truths repeat(ed.) *endlessly*… >

>Twisted-Truth(s) Open-ended…to: the-imag€(i)-nation…

<Rigged-Vote(s): closed. Ended. Statistics…and… >

<Dead-Weather *reports…as unpredictable as each-other.* >

>Without analysis. > knots of data and Trade-Mark patent mined controlled-by One-Firm Pirate-State(s) for a-time all proceeds kept all proceedings annulled obviously…

<Familyies' in-heritage heir-loom…

> African Black-Gold and shiny-White Diamonds stand-in for Money:

<See that *is* it…

Silicon: Creating Digital Markets (CDMs): empowering in-dividuals: available on commercial-terms to everyone:

<*That* is what You *work* with. > >Not just the-Money…you know?

< Just?

>Whatever: Stock-Good(s): and services' information: *you*-have:…

>Or: *think* I have? Get: my drift? >And there is a lot of it!

< Just-Ice?

>A Lo(0)t! Of it!

< No-more.

>And it has to be the correct-information. > Real? Evidence-based who checks simplifies amplifies

< Losing-It. Got-it! At last! The Good-Trade Truth! >

>Truth? > Ethical? > Morale Mod(e)ra(i)l? >

<Legitimate?… >

>Even? > Just…

>   < Tactical-Strateg(y)ies, written-down?

<Of-course! Even-handedness…

Screen-up:

>Rational-Regulatory: list…*endless*:

< Equitable. At least…

>Equitable: <Not!   >

<On the Open-*i*nformation Market(s) (O*i*M(s)) Kuwait-Iraq Saudi-Yemeni Syria-Iran Thailand-Malay Indian-China Australia to Nigeria to Brazil ancient foreign-Empires' reclaimed taking coalgasoil: shared.

< Tibet-Ukraine-Kashmir no-oil ancient-Empires' re-claiming food-basket >

<Believe-it…   > feel hard done-by dis-respect you do say I can't so I do dodo too in power-play two wrongs make two wrongs two rights make two rights too-many leave it there?

>Or not.   > Left. March…right:

<Not.   > right…people-paranoia! Given:

>*Soft-news…*

<Hard-News…   > to charm and almost-*paralyzed* with fear…and mis-placed awe, or not:

>Does anyone else know this?   >

<Global: Climate-Change: fragile-Democratic power-struggle oil-rigging…

> Consumer-vote? Nationalist-Authoritarian cult out of peoples' hands taken-back for one…

< Who has the-vote?

>Republic: Peoples' Populist(s): counted…under-threat! Given! Steal…

<Visa-Grad(e)Monarchial RE-xit: Presidentialist: may as well be would-be: investment-banker.

<For: One-Term

>2!

<3! Forever! >Input.

<Output.

> >For: Good-God?

<25%

➢ 12.5%

➢ 6.2.5%

Finite. In finityies'...

➢ 3.1.2.5%

➢ 1.5.5.1.2.5%

➢ 0.5.2.5.%

<Only un-reasonably un-ethically un-morally legitimately-*hypocritical*...

<Then?

Head-phoned sarcastically...scornfully-mordant liars saying your prayer(s) again surely? > for-given? Given conspiracy attacking hypocrisy crisis-safe online:

<Only: Natural of course. > Cultural-Monetising other hate&*fear common-sense* senses storm-trooped whimped whipped-up a *stale*-storm online:

>Well? <Of-course! > >Off- course.

<In the rough! >In the trough. >Out of bounds! >

<Prying… > powerless

>Nnnnnnnnnnnnnn…

The-Clerk looked-up: on-screen:

'Serious numbers! Quantum! I don't usually ask twice, but do You want me to take-a cut-in the recovery, eh? Cannot lose? Be-in on the next **Boom!** Basic-commodities' stocks&shares Quid Pro Quo?'

'Hard to get *Rare-Metal*s Hard-Wood RainForest-furniture…'

'There is more?'

'Rubber: flexible-plastid dig(i)-Silicon: Plastic frozen fluid hot-Oil and Gas under them there rocks passed generations metal-mineral: Generating-Energy: Fuel: based: Clean Uranium. Plutonium…'

'*Polonium*? Novo-cheque. Industrial: *or* Military-use?'

'Business. To be *had*? Mining-minerals from The Earth. From Space? Eh? Satellites and Solar-panels perhaps?'

'Who knows? Exciting-*possibilities…*'

'…and we do not think we have to be persuaded. Know what I mean? Just a simple 'Yes' is all 'We' need.' 'Who doesn't?'

'For a *comfortable*-Peace?'

'Piece? Of What@*Never…*'

'Never say: Never!'

'*What*?'

'Why-not? Trade…Shopping-War(s):...'

'Then. All the Time! That is War? Shopping?'

'Is it?'

'Buying and selling…'

'Time?'

'Work-Share?'

'Gold-Currencyies' Credits. Our-Selves. Buying and selling constant movement…'

'Until now stopped?'

'Life is just a Game to be Won! With the most NNN/nnn…'

'Not: with the least nnn/NNN?'

'N/n…' *at the end of the Game: Green-washed Golf&Gold Capital Town&Countryies' Sport(s): the end unknown in ad-vance: when the end is known in advance overly drama-tic all rights on the night!*

'Tonight?'

'You-Lose! Always death even(tu)ally.'

'Staged?'

'Some people want to die so they can be-free.'

'Can any-one be free?'

'Not: of-war. Or Peace. Why would you not-w*ant* Peace?'

'Like we had before *this haha*?!'

'Like we had before *this*…This-time. Last-Time: Cannot have *the*-same-again, ever.'

'Every time…is…'

'Different? Of-course.'

'Equity-only…' v*irtually-preserved…*

'Inequitably advanced defended by this: *sullen*-Madness! Mutually Assisted. Destruction…'

'MAD? *Assured?*'

'Never.'

'Happens.'

'Insured? You? Think you are. No. You're…' *breaking-points snapped! broken, into-pieces:*

'The-Whole-Thing! Capital-Equity: collapsed…'

'Crashed prices no good for buyer or seller.'

'Whether-designed to or not-to…'

'With: Iconic-Catastrophic damage…'

'For *some-Sector(s):…*'

'All!'

'Ignored.'

'Ig-snored…'

'Not-All. See?'

'Cannot-be?'

'Again? Yet?'

Looking-out. Farms&Suburban-edges trimmed-hedges garden up to overgrown woods and peeling whitewash walls. Compound 3 or 4 storied building and alongside creosote-fences graffiti-walls enclosed-ditch between poplar and ash-growing pastures and soon to be harvested-fields. By the Railway-Track…looking-out:

'In-Equitably Killing-Field(s)…'

'For: Meat&Harvest food in: Country-Town…' *urbane.*

'Urban. Petty-Bourg(e) Town. Cit(y)(i)(€)s…'

'Business-All. Expense of all else. Thank You Staff Workers Army Customers exploited…aquired…debased.'

Ch(e)at-Cat. Nascent competition: out-doing and adding to: bought-out merged…

Monopoly-Corporate Capital-Merger: WhatsApp? AWS Alphabet and

InstaGram Medical-Advice and Check-Up: Educational: Numeracy literacy reaction redaction speed rate(s): Space National Country-Wide and Global Government and Corporate-Scientific: Empire: Driven Test-Lift-Off: ex-ploded in *flame*(s): cleared-land for sheep-people cattle-drovers off the-land drifting carbon-cloud fumes …

Forest-Fire Sale(s): Flood-Damage: *swamping*-ancestor(y):

HQ-Office: in every-City, or the Love, every Country of:

The Globe. Passed through and beyond…

'The-City@Business as Usual!'

'So…'

'Stupid! Damn-lies…'

''Half-Lies. Unchecked re-peated endlessly…'

'Half-truths. Innovating nothing but lies, the real innovators go-by bought-off…elaborated on as speculative reckonings in whose favour?'

'Telegraphed-Times Mail-Express Post…'

'Until now…'

'It was all going so well…'

'Ostrich-Head in the sand…'

'So, you knew?'

'What? In the water…'

'Of course…Boarding: *Statistic(*s): NNN/nnn…weather-reports as reliable as the day before…as un-predictable as each-other without proper-*analysis*.'

'See that it is…*that* is what You have to work with…Red-Barbarian at the Gate! Red-Menace to be-destroyed at-will. The Big Green-Giant Hulk! Criminal-Collective! The Junior-Justice Party Patriarchal-President Monarchical…'

'Place-Marker: Ruler…'

'Man in The High-Castle.'

'And it is always…fraternising Big-Man cannot stand to be alone…'

Tuned-out turned: *away and down into the-screen*:

'Playing the-Game@orchestrated-violence Big-Media: lies paid-off with real-lives…'

'Single-Partyies' B*luey*-Meanie: insect-farm fund-raising wily-Fox

Government…'

'Crackdown on tax-evasion and avoidance.'

'Corruption. Fraud. More-lies not even covered-tracks to in-still *fear*…terror.'

'Special-operations like friendly-fire!'

'Sanctioning-fraud trusting brass-plate oligarch-banking golden-passbook

financial citizenship special if you like…'

'Crop-steal: Island-bases spread-out across the globe.'

'Off-Shore Banking-Robbery…'

'As a soldier looting Police and Thieves!'

'People. Killing.'

'Dis-claiming de-claiming: sue *them!*'

'Accidental-Damage!'

'Kickin' the Can.'

'Down the Road: Next-Generation BRIG-Bank…

'Sailing-BLOCs…'

'Shipped as Flagged. Troll Fleet-Expedient:'

'Low2No taxes or regulation Government People personally-Pragmatic.'

'For: Fair?'

'For: Rich.'

Brick-*Bat* Re-(IR.)Gulated Utilities (URU) a-*twittering*:' in-formation:

'Socially…'

'Innovative.' *spirit: lobbying-cronyism: news-media corps.*

Seen:

'*Hoax*-loan: and *overdraft*:…a-greed regardless of in-coming…'

'The-*Gambler* bets on what they *think may happen*. The Banker on what has only just happened a pica-second ago…'

'That *others* do not know.'

'Are not *meant* to know…'

'Yet.' *Con-cierge-Conscience Customer? Share-holder? Business-hush-hush…clandestine…covert…confidential The-People! Are not meant to know?*

'Playing-the-Tables…and all the Chairs and Tables of all those Generation(s)' Society?'

'There is no such thing as Society. There are only individuals and families…'

‘National-Socialism is…’

‘The problem with Socialism: is:

‘You eventually run out of other peoples’ money to spend…’

‘Investment-Capitalisms’ problem is…same! You run out of other peoples’ disposable income. Other Peoples’ Money to invest.’ With an air of *un*-fulfilled un-*done*:

‘To: spend. Get *in-early*…get-out.’

>R/E:…loading:…soon…sooner…

<Inter: National: Corporate-Governance: *Own-banking currency(ies): listing:…*

>The International-Conference: *insider-information: ...*

‘What if *they don’t decide?* Done-dealing?’

‘Never! Could not-stop ourselves, could we? ‘It’…was just…too-Good! To be-True!’

‘The-Truth?’

‘Fair-Fee Charge (FFC).’

‘Customer-Ownership: owing: N.n:…’

‘Data and Pay: De-liver(y): Logistic(s): Nation-State: Pro_duct: tape:

‘Game-Over.’

‘Enviably too-Big to Fail!’

‘The rest of Us?’

‘Too small to survive?’

‘Society?’

‘Politics of Envy.’

‘You too?’ *envied all the same...*

'Only, arguably…'

'Enemyies'…'

'Too Bad…'

'To: Fail.' To: fall…

'Only *winning*-bids now…'

'Fixed.' *assuming:* ab-solution: latest Savings&Loans' scandal…

'Lion-roars! when it gets hungry!' *roaming…re-connecting…*

'These Lion-*Loans* then?'

'Dragon-Debt: You sign for them:…'

'Credit-Cow:…'

'Entre-preneur between government-bank-loan and the gutter…'

Online…

''We' have agreed the 'same' documented agreements?'

'Morally-Mal-efficient?'

'Legally Mor(E)(T)-*Ally legalese…'*

*'Legislat(e)d.)4b*oth ambitious as ambiguous:…'

'E-motional:-E-th(n)ic(s): dis-*posable each-of-us…'*

< Victim-Villain re-sponds: Hyper-Heroic con.traryies' c*alculator*: **NNN/nnn**….un-fair fair-ground tourist-attraction *digital sig(n)ature pass/word vault…safe…grift…graft…for-ever?*

Science and technology[edit]

- Graft (surgery), a surgical procedure
- Grafting, the joining of plant tissues
- Grafting (chemistry), chemical modification of surface
- Grafting (decision trees), in computer science, adding nodes
- to a decision tree

- Graft (politics), a form of political corruption.
- Graft (work) to work hard at something put in the effort.

Grift may refer to:

- (Grift) Confidence trick swindle
- (Grift) to obtain money immorally or through deceitful
- means.

(thanks to Wikipedia.com Wikimedia.com Merriam-Webster Collins

etymology thesaurus)

Also by M.Stow:

WarFair4.2: Rogue-Citizen: *Into The Abyss*...Global-Citizen

WarFair4.3: Local-Den(i)Zen...

Walter Mepham (A First World War true family and personal stories)

EarthCentre:The End of the Universe (An Anthropic Odyssey)

Universal Verses

Pan Tan-Gou

Arctol & other short novels, stories and poetry...

Standard Oil Co. (by Pablo Neruda, Canto General, 1940)

When the drill bored down toward the stony fissures
and plunged its implacable intestine
into the subterranean estates,
and dead years, eyes of the ages,
imprisoned plants' roots
and scaly systems
became strata of water,
fire shot up through the tubes
transformed into cold liquid,
in the customs house of the heights,
issuing from its world of sinister depth,
it encountered a pale engineer
and a title deed.

However entangled the petroleum's arteries may be,
however the layers may change their silent site
and move their sovereignty amid the earth's bowels,
when the fountain gushes its paraffin foliage,
Standard Oil arrived beforehand
with its checks and it guns,
with its governments and its prisoners.

Their obese emperors from New York
are suave smiling assassins
who buy silk, nylon, cigars
petty tyrants and dictators.
They buy countries, people, seas, police, county councils,
distant regions where the poor hoard their corn
like misers their gold:
Standard Oil awakens them,
clothes them in uniforms, designates
which brother (sic!) is the enemy.

The Paraguayan fights its war,
and the Bolivian wastes away
in the jungle with its machine gun.

A President assassinated for a drop of petroleum,
a million-acre mortgage,
a swift execution on a morning mortal with light, petrified,

a new prison camp for subversives,
in Patagonia, a betrayal, scattered shots
beneath a petroliferous moon,
a subtle change of ministers
in the capital, a whisper
like an oil tide,
and zap, you'll see
how Standard Oil's letters shine above the clouds,
above the seas, in your home,
illuminating their dominions.

Ubuntu: I am because we are

I am because you are

In a country well governed, poverty is something to be ashamed of. In a country badly governed, wealth is something to be ashamed of. *Confucius (551-479 before modern era).*

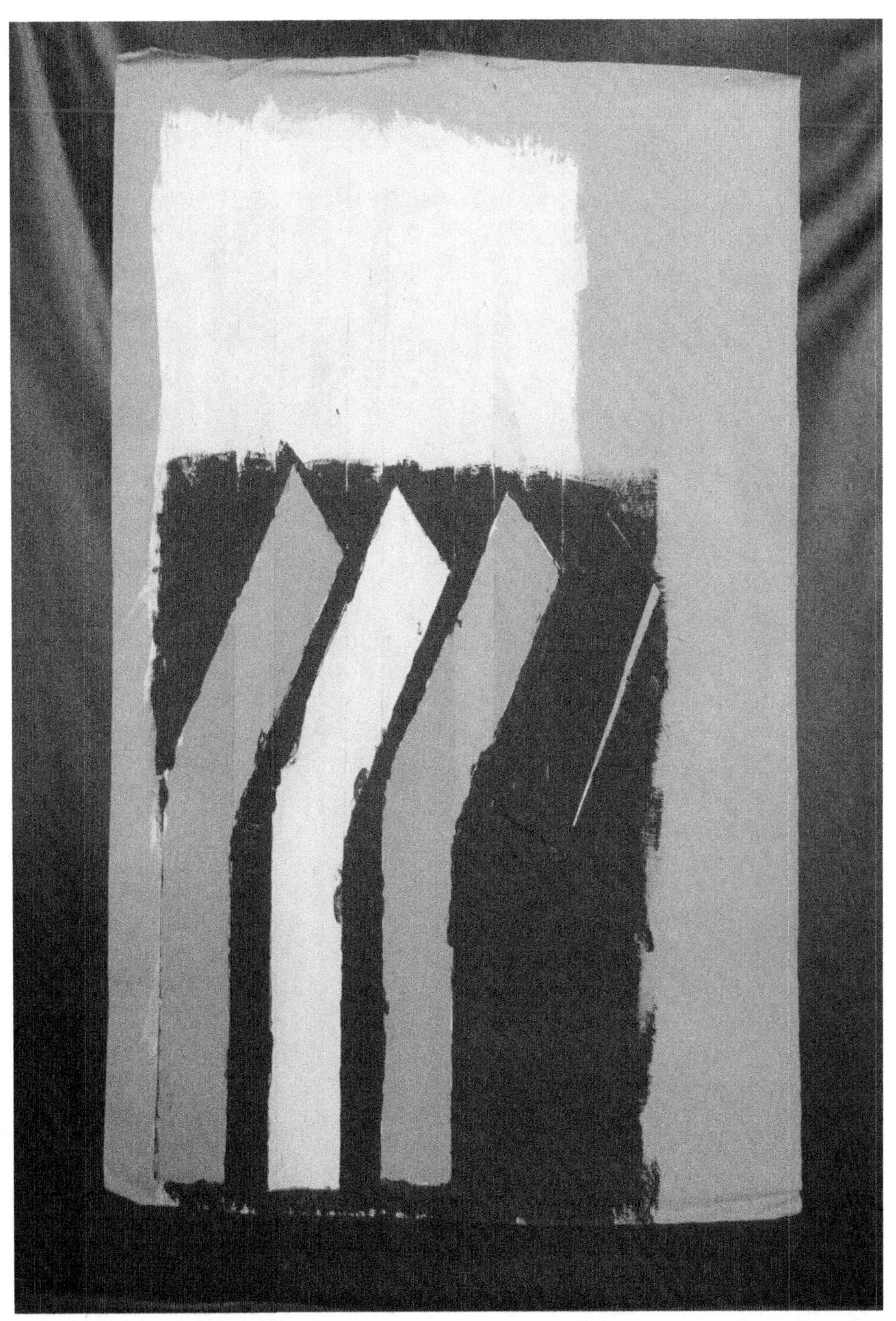

WF4.155.

WF4.156.

https://www.amazon.co.uk/God-We-Trust-Jean-Shepherd/dp/0385021747

https://www.ibm.com/blogs/nordic-msp/in-god-we-trust-all-others-must-bring-data/

https://www.investopedia.com/terms/a/animal-spirits.asp